Praise for
SHAKING IN THE FOREST

"*Shaking in the Forest* is so much more than a career journey—it is a courageous look at life lessons from several different perspectives. If you like to read about fascinating calls in the responder world, or you want to learn the mental and emotional processes that help a person grow and survive, or you want to hear about the meaning and life lessons we all can learn from experiences, whether they are our own or someone else's, this book is for you. I am already planning when I will read it a second time so I can again visit lessons on courage, hope, learning, fear, compassion, and so much more."

—DR. MARY SCHOENFELDT, FACULTY, FEMA EMERGENCY MANAGEMENT INSTITUTE

"The author, a self-described systems thinker and student of chaos theory, shares her thoughts on her lifetime of work in emergency services. Reading *Shaking in the Forest* is like starting an internet search and creating multiple open tabs—it's all interesting and it's all connected in an overarching way to the unifying theme of how seeing the worst of life opens our eyes to what is best and beautiful."

—JENNIFER E. HASSEL, AUTHOR OF *BADASS GRIEF*

"Lori Hodges immediately captivates readers from the start of *Shaking in the Forest*. She quietly lets the audience into her raw, personal stories and reflections, resulting in unpredictable experiences we can all learn from. Lori's resilience in every aspect of her life—from personal challenges and struggles to her time as a firefighter, paramedic, and emergency manager—is not only inspirational but gripping and moving, showing her heartfelt passion for helping others. She shares the good, the bad, and the chaos. Her 'fight or flee' mentality stirs many human emotions and has not stopped Lori from looking ahead with a positive attitude. The life lessons spotlighted throughout the

book are extraordinary."
—LETITIA (TISH) E. HART, DEACON, AND AUTHOR OF *REACH OUT WITH ACTS OF KINDNESS: A GUIDE TO HELPING OTHERS IN CRISIS*

"Lori's personal journey makes a captivating and compelling read. Lori opens her guarded heart, pouring her experiences, life's challenges, metaphysical learning, and philosophical insights onto every page. She provides a transformative journey into the depths of her consciousness. Her prose provides humorous yet profound insights that guide readers toward a state of inner peace and presence that is both liberating and empowering. This story reminds me of Eckart Tolle's *The Power of Now* in its delivery of embracing the present moment fully, without judgment or resistance.

This is not a story of Lori's work as a firefighter, paramedic, and emergency manager, although she weaves in experiences of calls and incidents, but a story of trauma, perseverance, resilience, and self-actualization at a time of another unwelcome affliction. Each page is imbued with the pain and beauty of growth, making it not only a memoir but also a guide on how to confront one's past and shape one's future. I found Lori's story remarkably similar to my own, making it easily relatable. I highly recommend it for anyone ready to embark on a journey of self-discovery and inner transformation."
—TINA BYNUM, HOMELAND SECURITY FACULTY, WESTERN CONNECTICUT STATE UNIVERSITY

"This book is a treasure trove of profound insights into the complexities of life and death, personal and professional growth, and bestows the simple to complex challenges faced in a world of chaos and disorder. One of the standout qualities of this book is the vivid imagery that paints a rich and emotional landscape. This collection of personal experiences is a deeply personal exploration of Lori's own journey, which adds an authentic and relatable dimension to the story. *Shaking in the Forest* is a book that will leave an indelible mark on your heart and mind."

—**KIMBERLY CAMPBELL,
PARAMEDIC, FIREFIGHTER,
AND EMERGENCY MANAGER**

"Lori has an impressive background and a world of knowledge. Her book shows that anything is possible – if you try, you can succeed. As a retired responder, I was able to relate to her emotions and thinking. I feel some of us are destined to do the work we do, even to be that "black cloud." This book is from the heart and direct. It will let people who read it know what the life of a responder is really like."

—**RANDY COUNCELL,
DIRECTOR OF SAFETY AND SECURITY (RETIRED),
CHERRY CREEK SCHOOL DISTRICT**

"I truly connected with this well-told story. The EMS-specific portions are not overly long and are perfect for both those in the emergency services and lay people as well. This is a book for people searching for clarity in their lives, no matter their life experience. It's a brilliant text to help a reader find an ah-ha moment."

—**CHARLES LOPEZ, FIREFIGHTER AND EMS RESPONDER**

"*Shaking in the Forest* is funny at times, sad at other times, and will cause readers to reflect on their own lives, which I think is outstanding. Lori discusses real life tragedies in both a critical dark side but also with the real human side and includes humor as needed."

—**MIKE GAVIN,
BATTALION CHIEF AND EMERGENCY MANAGER (RETIRED),
POUDRE FIRE AUTHORITY**

"Lori is resilience personified. She has taken every challenge thrown her way (neglect, abuse, loss, and disease) and turned them into posttraumatic growth opportunities. Not only did she grow from her experiences, she turned them into tools of selfless service for her community. This book is truly inspiring for those who face the darkness every day. Thank you, Lori, for your courage to be vulnerable and for sharing your journey. Your story is lifesaving."

—MARC BAKER, THE BAKER'S DOZEN, EMERGENCY MANAGEMENT NETWORK

Shaking in the Forest:
Finding Light in the Darkness

by Lori Renee Hodges

© Copyright 2024 Lori Renee Hodges

ISBN 979-8-88824-400-5

All rights reserved. No part of this publication may be reproduced, stored in a retrieval system, or transmitted in any form or by any means—electronic, mechanical, photocopy, recording, or any other—except for brief quotations in printed reviews, without the prior written permission of the author.

Published by

◂köehlerbooks™

3705 Shore Drive
Virginia Beach, VA 23455
800-435-4811
www.koehlerbooks.com

Shaking in the Forest

Finding Light in the Darkness

SHAKING IN THE FOREST

FINDING LIGHT IN THE DARKNESS

Lori Renee Hodges

VIRGINIA BEACH
CAPE CHARLES

To Mom, who told me there is nothing I cannot do and who showed me how to be courageous in the face of fear, and to Tammie, who wouldn't let me run away and who would help me bury a body with no questions asked.

Content Warning

This book describes multiple emergency calls by paramedics, as well as personal recollections from childhood trauma. Content includes topics such as suicide, sexual assault, domestic violence, child abuse, and other general trauma.

Introduction

"**I smell fuel.**"

"Stop!" The team leader raised his hand in the air. "Quiet."

We stopped walking, and everyone listened intently. All that could be heard for several seconds was the sound of the forest.

"Spread out everyone into a line search. We're close to the wreckage, so keep your eyes open."

The search-and-rescue team continued methodically hiking through the forest and farther up the mountain as the scent of aviation fuel grew stronger. After about fifteen minutes of climbing, a faint outline of two people could be seen in the distance walking toward us.

As they got closer, I searched for possible injuries or bleeding, but the only thing I noticed was the enormous smiles on both the men's faces.

"Boy are we glad to see you guys," one of the men stated, visibly tired but relieved.

Both pilots looked relatively unscathed. The odor of fuel fell heavily around us in the forest as we talked with the two-person crew of the single-engine Cessna that had crashed in the woods nearby. I remained stunned that the men we were talking to had both just survived a plane crash. The wreckage was found about a quarter-mile away, buried in a dense area of the forest.

This was my first plane crash and my first search-and-rescue mission. I was thirteen years old.

In all my years of working through disasters, the phrase I have heard the most is, "I just didn't think this would happen to me." I also have a sneaking feeling that the media has an ongoing bet to see which outlet can get the first person to say, "Why would God let bad things happen to good people?"

I am not that person.

I am the person who plans for the worst-case scenario as part of my normal routine because, from everything I have seen, bad things clearly happen to everyone—whether they're "good" or not. One universal truth is that we will all face both beauty and tragedy in our lives. If we live, we must also eventually face death. We will see unimaginable cruelty, destruction, and loss and will see both the best and the worst of humanity if we are privileged enough to live a long life.

With all the tragedy and loss, there is also exceptional beauty in the world, and it is often because of the loss that we stop, take a breath, and see the beauty when it occurs. We read the story of the young nineteen-year-old who risked his own life to save another from a fiery auto accident. We witness thousands of people gather in solidarity to call for change after an injustice led to tragedy. We take the time to watch the magnificent sunrise that was only possible due to the wildfire burning in a nearby forest. Through it all, the profoundly good days start to mean so much. Those are the days when you gather with family and friends and tell stories and laugh, remembering other good times from the past. The births, birthdays, reunions, awards, and graduations bring such delight, pure joy, and pride. They are all so much better because we know that those moments in time are precious. If we are lucky, we have more good days than bad, and we get the chance to live a long life filled with beautiful moments and memories.

At the age of twenty-five, I chose a career in tragedy. Unlike many who avoid the worst life has to offer, I chose to make a career out of terrible days in people's lives. I have spent the last twenty-five years in emergency services—first as a firefighter and paramedic and later as an emergency manager helping to coordinate the response to and recovery from disasters. It is through this work that I have come to see the beauty in tragedy.

I have watched people react to life's miseries and bad days in various ways. I have seen someone completely fall apart over a cut on their arm that will leave a scar, and I have seen another brave through the pain of cancer without taking pain medications so that they can visit with their children with a clear head while in the hospital. The brave ones wondered why these things had happened, but they also made a conscious decision to keep moving forward. They come to a point where they stop, stand up, dust themselves off, and take that one small step forward that is needed to begin living life again.

The majority of my life has been ruled by my amygdala, the small part of my brain that creates the fight-or-flight response. I learned about fear as a child. I initially trusted that I could depend upon my family as a stable constant and that friends and neighbors would not harm me, but bad things did happen. Alcoholism crept into my family dynamic, shifting stability to dread. Drug use destroyed high school friends, and later, abuse became more than something that happens to other people. Insecurity took hold, and with each new trust-breaking experience, those childhood fears took root, grew, and decided to stay awhile.

Paramedicine allowed me to face many of my fears, but it also reminded me of why I had fears in the first place. Any call could bring forth a memory or reality I was hesitant to revisit but forced to in order to help the patient. There are many things I learned as a paramedic, but how to both brace for fear and face it at the same time was probably the most valuable.

A picture on my wall at work reminds me that chaos is where great dreams begin. It is where we are shaken out of our daily stupor with a force that rattles the walls and screams in our ear, "Wake up!" Chaos forces all of us to look at life differently. We face what we have never faced before, causing us to find new solutions to new challenges. And with each event something is learned that gets deeply embedded inside the files of our mind. This leads to lessons for the future, creates greater empathy for others, and provides inner strength that helps us get through future life challenges.

Just as everything slows down and quiets in times of crisis, allowing you to use all your senses to respond, we sometimes need to look around and see what the world is trying to teach us. And after years as an emergency responder and emergency manager, I find this truer now than ever before.

While paramedicine taught me about facing my fears, becoming an emergency manager taught me to cherish the chaos that is life. I believe that it is through chaos that we become the people we were meant to be. It's called a life-altering event for a reason. We can let that event define us and cause us to become smaller, or we can let it teach us something and rise. There is such great potential for a shift of monumental proportions in how we live, how we work, what we care about, and who we care about. The very worst thing that could happen after a chaotic event is for everyone to just wish that we go back to normal—that we close our eyes and refuse to learn anything from such a time.

Open your eyes.

Look into the darkness, and I promise you will see a light that will guide you to better things to come. It is all a matter of our ability to both embrace the darkness and let it go when the time is right. Knowing that the strength to recover is there gives me the hope I need that I will be one of those who can stand up, brush myself off, and take that first step to face a new day.

PHASE 1:
GROWING

I cannot stop your spiral, but I can wrap my arms around you until it begins to make sense. I cannot drown out the voices in your head, but I can whisper it's okay until they fade. I am not afraid of your darkness. I do not despise your mess. I fear your inability to see what I see, a beautiful soul.

—JM Storm

CHAPTER 1

DEATH

"**Hey, Honeybucket.**"

I rolled my eyes at the nickname my brother Kent used. He had just gotten a sweet cherry-red Camaro for his sixteenth birthday, so he had been tasked with giving me a ride home from a Civil Air Patrol meeting at our high school. My first car was an old clunker that honked every time I turned left. But, no, I'm not at all bitter.

I reached out my hand to grab the door handle, but just before I could open the door, Kent hit the gas, and the car lurched forward several feet. I tried again, and he gunned the engine again. This sadistic torment continued while he laughed hysterically until he knew I was about to snap.

When I was finally allowed to get into the car, I waved goodbye to my friends, and we pulled out of the school parking lot, turning right onto Highway 83. My friend Kate was in front of us with her father behind the wheel of his pickup truck as we headed in the direction of the town of Parker.

In 1988, Highway 83 was two lanes that stretched from Colorado Springs through Parker. It traveled up and over the rolling hills east of Denver. As we drove, Kate and her father crested a hill and disappeared from view.

Then everything went still. Each action occurred in slow motion as my brother hit the brakes and brought the Camaro to a stop.

Dust hung in the air, slowly falling to the ground. Vehicles were stopped in front of us.

Everything was silent.

I have thought about this in times when people say their life passes before their eyes or when everything slows almost to a stop. I believe it is the brain trying to comprehend everything that is happening and due to the importance of it all, it seems as if time has slowed because the brain is taking everything in. I believe that the brain also starts flipping through files of past experiences to see if it can find anything it can use to help in the current situation. Our life is literally passing before our eyes as our brain tries to solve a new problem.

Two vehicles had crashed head-on at high speed. The first was a four-door sedan with one passenger that ended up on the side of the road along the dirt shoulder. The other was the pickup truck with Kate and her father. Vehicle debris littered the highway on both sides, effectively cutting off access. Long black tire marks were etched across the road.

My brother and I were the first on the scene.

I jumped out of the car and ran toward Kate and her father. On the way, as if in slow motion, I looked to my left as I passed the other car and saw the driver sitting behind the wheel, head turned toward me, unconscious, with blood running down his face. Kate had an injury to her wrist but otherwise seemed fine. Her father, on the other hand, was gravely injured. The engine compartment had been pushed into the driver's side, impaling him. He was alive when I walked up to the vehicle but did not stay conscious for long. I made eye contact with him and just knew he wasn't going to be coming home. I leaned into the driver's compartment with my arms on the door frame. We spoke briefly, him asking me to take care of his daughter. I did my best to calm his anxiety and assured him that Kate would be all right. We would take care of her.

My brother and I stayed until an ambulance arrived and then helped Kate to my brother's car to take her into town. Kate's father died that night in his truck from a drunk driver who had swerved into his lane.

DEATH AND UNCERTAINTY have been a part of my life for quite some time. I first really started paying attention to this in 2012, when ten family members and friends died in that short twelve-month period. As each new month brought more bad news, I looked back and realized that death really wasn't a stranger. I'd wager not a lot of other people started their teens searching for downed aircraft in the forest. And, I went to high school off a road nicknamed "Death Highway" because of how many kids died on that two-lane highway every year.

Death has been around me for some time.

Ever since I can remember, I have thought I would die young. When I was a young girl, I would blindfold myself and walk through the house just to see if I could get around if ever I went blind. I felt compelled to plan so I could successfully maneuver the stairs and the multiple knee-crushing pieces of furniture throughout our home. I did the same with crutches just in case I broke a leg. The presence of alcoholism in my family definitely played a role in my constant fear of the unknown. Throughout several generations, alcoholism had ended lives and caused havoc. You could say that I came out of the womb ready for the bottom to drop out.

My amygdala has had a front row seat in my life for a very long time, keeping me alert to all the dangers of the world while also preparing me to fight or flee depending upon the threat. I lived my early life as if I might die at any moment, and I always had something horrible swimming around in my head—the uncertainty of life and its dangers. I was convinced I would never make it out of my teens. Upon graduating from high school, my one and only goal was to move somewhere new and make it on my own. Again, I had the fear that if I depended upon anyone, I would put myself at risk. In 1989, I moved to Las Vegas, Nevada with three hundred dollars in my pocket. I quickly got a job, began living my adult life, and later was astonished when I made it through my twenties and then my thirties relatively unscathed. Not only had I made it through each decade, but I also remained healthy and strong.

For my fortieth birthday, I declared that the next decade would be the finest of them all—my fearless forties! I would conquer my long-held fears of the future and no longer think the worst.

The universe was listening. She responded by declaring, "Challenge accepted!"

I let my guard down.

This was a mistake.

At the age of forty-three, I attended a Naval Postgraduate School program that brought me to California for two weeks each quarter. During one of those trips, around November, I developed great anxiety. A million butterflies swarmed in my stomach and chest, and my heart began to race. I tried to relax and get some sleep, hoping it would pass, but to no avail. I even thought about canceling my flight and taking a different one on the chance that this was a sign from above that danger lurked on the arranged flight. But while away, my dog had gotten into a fight with another dog, and she was injured badly. I really wanted to get home and see her to make sure everything was okay.

The anxiety grew during my layover in Los Angeles and continued throughout the final leg of my journey to Denver. Once I got my bags from the baggage claim and took the shuttle to my car, I knew something wasn't right. The anxiety continued to increase, and the fluttering of butterflies in my chest became a physical pain.

I felt a moment's relief when I finally arrived home and greeted my bandaged dog, seeing that she was injured but strong. She would recover. But as I took the stairs up to my room to lie down, I became short of breath, and the discomfort in my chest increased. I just wanted to get to my bed and lie down. It would all be okay if I could just get some rest now that I had gotten home safely. But the discomfort turned to chest pressure and finally developed into pain in my jaw and my left arm.

It doesn't take an ex-medic to know those signs and symptoms are really bad. So, ten minutes after arriving home, I got up, kissed my dogs, and got into my car to drive to the emergency room. Why I didn't think to call an ambulance, I have no idea. I just knew I needed to get to the ER as soon as possible, and my car was in the garage. I left quickly. All my symptoms screamed heart attack.

I didn't have to wait long in the ER waiting room. Anyone with these types of symptoms is usually rushed to a room. And by this time, I was so short of breath I could only provide one-word answers (another red flag). I had thought more about the symptoms on my way to the hospital, so when the nurses and doctors came in to evaluate my condition, I said two words, "pulmonary embolism."

Luckily, the hospital staff trusted my assessment, immediately did a bunch of tests and gave me some medicine to help with the anxiety that comes with the inability to breathe. I quickly texted my mom to let her know what had happened and to see if she could help me with my dogs in case I remained in the hospital or in case I did not make it out of the ER. One out of three people who get a pulmonary embolism, or PE, does not survive. I knew the seriousness of the condition.

I had thought I had felt fear prior to this incident. I had thought I knew what anxiety felt like. But nothing in my life had prepared me for the inability to breathe. I couldn't speak or communicate effectively. And that feeling that I wouldn't make it out of the hospital was pervasive. Knowing I was facing death and knowing it could be imminent was excruciating.

The tests confirmed that I had a long blood clot that went from my ankle to my thigh. A cluster of blood clots had broken away from that large blood clot in my left leg and traveled up into my lungs, scattering them with multiple blockages, making it impossible to breathe. The embolism had caused strain on my heart, literally causing a heart attack.

All my old fears and thoughts about my mortality slammed back into my brain. The short nap my amygdala had taken was immediately interrupted and she was back in the game! This was proof that letting my guard down would only lead to chaos and trouble. Better to live in a state of hypervigilance than allow something like this to catch me off guard again.

The doctors and nurses quickly started to treat me with clot busters and blood thinners, and once stabilized, I was transferred from the emergency room to the Intensive Care Unit, where I spent the next several days. Luckily, I was not one of the three that dies from an embolism. I survived. But in the coming days, I had to welcome in anxiety and fear again. At the beginning of my fearless forties, I had been brutally reminded of the fragility of life, and I could no longer ignore my long-held fears that tragedy was around the corner, just waiting to strike.

The anxiety that goes along with experiencing a PE is excruciating, and once the clot is resolved, it doesn't go away for most patients. Each day following my hospital stay, I wondered if another clot would form. I went to the emergency room a few times in the next twelve months, thinking something was dreadfully wrong, only to be told that everything looked good. My doctors explained about the lingering anxiety and said it could last for months following a hospitalization. The thought of having another embolism caused me great worry.

The tightening of my chest and the increasing heartbeat.

The inability to take a breath.

The deep anxiety.

The feeling that Death was standing by my side, just waiting for the last breath to finish so that he could take me. The very real fear that each minute would be my last.

CHAPTER 2

BIRTH

DROWNINGS ARE MORE common than you would think. According to the Centers for Disease Control and Prevention, there is an average of 3,536 fatal unintentional drownings annually in the United States—about ten deaths per day. And one in five people who die from drowning are children fourteen and younger.

My first drowning call as a paramedic was for a baby who had fallen into a pool when her parents weren't looking. It was a simple thing. One minute is all it took for the baby to get close to the edge of the pool and fall in. It was another minute before anyone realized what had happened.

Getting a 911 call on a baby in distress is one of the worst a paramedic can get. No call rivals the stress of holding a child's life in your hands. My partner and I knew going into the call that a bad outcome was likely. We prepared mentally as much as possible before arriving on scene.

The minute the ambulance stopped along the curb next to the home, the mother came running out of the house clutching the lifeless baby. I had barely stepped out of the ambulance when she practically threw the baby at me. I cradled the baby safely in my arms and looked down. The small one was limp, a light shade of blue, and not breathing.

I jumped in the back of the ambulance to begin my work. I sat on the bench seat and began CPR. As I secured the baby on my right arm, I gently rested my hand on her chest. From that small bit of pressure, water flowed out of her mouth in a gush, clearing her lungs. She slowly began breathing on her own again. Nothing invasive, no CPR, just a hand on her chest. Before the mom jumped into the back of the ambulance and we headed to the hospital, the baby started to cry.

It was the most beautiful sound in the world.

I HAVE ALWAYS been attracted to emergency work but did not see it as a life's calling until my midtwenties. I joined the Civil Air Patrol at thirteen years old because I wanted to learn how to fly airplanes. But through the years, I found I was more drawn to ground search-and-rescue activities, where we searched for downed aircraft and missing people, and it was okay to get a little dirty. I never thought it was strange to be a teenager walking through the forest to find plane wreckage. I merely found it to be a decent way to spend my time.

But my life's work did not truly begin until 1995, when I was stopped at a stoplight, waiting to move forward. As I waited, I realized my life was on hold. I had moved to Las Vegas straight out of high school, ready to make my way in the world. I worked odd jobs, went to classes occasionally, and hung out with new friends. By 1995, I had spent six years wandering and muddling through. I didn't know where I belonged or what I wanted to do. I took a college course here and there at the University of Nevada Las Vegas, but they mainly consisted of subjects like running or racquetball, and they were so haphazard that there would be no way to string them together into any type of degree. I also bounced around from job to job, looking for something I enjoyed but never really finding my niche. I went out with friends every night, drinking and playing pool—having a lot of fun but no closer to figuring out if there was a purpose at all for my existence.

At that moment, while stopped at the light, an ambulance came screeching past with lights on and the siren wailing. I felt a strong jolt to the body, suddenly seeing a path forward. I am a superstitious sort and one who believes strongly in signs. The ambulance passing at the exact time I contemplated my life was a sign.

Unlike most decisions, where I jump in immediately with both feet, lacking the patience to wait, I decided to take a bit of time to ensure this was the correct path. That coming weekend I had friends coming into town from Colorado to attend three days of Grateful Dead shows in Vegas, giving me the perfect opportunity for relaxation and reflection.

While at the second day of the shows, a woman standing in front of me decided to take acid for the first time. Instead of the positive experience she had hoped for, she had a visit from a bunch of demons and ultimately fell to the ground in a seizure. At the time, I had little medical training past basic first aid and CPR, so I merely protected her head from banging against the metal railing near her body until the medics could get to her.

The Grateful Dead had their own medics that toured with them, so when they arrived, I followed them as they carried her to the medical area within the stadium. I wanted to see how they worked. I was in awe. Each paramedic worked with the injured and ill—most of them there because of willingly consuming massive amounts of drugs. I spent a few hours watching as concertgoers came and went. The helpers had only one mission, and that was to do what was needed to get people well. There was no judgment. Many in the medical area had overdosed on some type of drug or were intoxicated beyond measure, but the single-minded approach of each paramedic was to get everyone feeling good again so that they could enjoy the show, perhaps a bit wiser than before.

As I watched the medics work, I clearly saw paramedicine as my path. I had found the sign I had asked for, and who would have thought it would be in the form of a gift from the Grateful Dead?

Within one month, I moved back to Colorado and enrolled in EMT school. My life had finally begun.

I can honestly say the Grateful Dead saved my life.

CHAPTER 3
The Unknown

"You can come in nonemergent. One patient. DOA."

My partner switched off the lights and siren, and we slowed the ambulance slightly as we moved out of Breckenridge and up the mountain. The call was a one-vehicle accident on Hoosier Pass, a typical call for a cold winter night with icy roads.

Once we arrived, the firefighters on the scene told us that the patient had been ejected from the vehicle and had been found in the forest down the embankment. Looking around the scene, I noticed that the contents of the vehicle were scattered in a large debris field around the forest. The car had flipped and ejected everything within, including my patient.

"Are you certain there was only one person in the car?" I asked the firefighters.

They assured me that they had searched the forest and found no other victims, so I grabbed the cardiac monitor and some basic supplies and trekked down the slope to where I found a twenty-something-year-old male lying on the ground surrounded by the darkness of the forest. My first reaction was surprise. I was struck by the fact that my patient didn't have a scratch on him. He looked like he was sleeping, just taking a nap in the woods. But his eyes were open, staring blankly up at the stars.

I knelt down, checked his carotid pulse, and checked for breathing. Finding nothing, I hooked him up to the cardiac monitor to confirm death. At about the same time, I heard a faint moan come from the forest behind me.

I turned around quickly to see what had joined me in the forest. My instinct and intuition spiked, but as I searched the forest, all I saw was the night darkness and shadows through the trees. My partner slowly side-stepped down the hill toward me, so I asked her if she had heard anything.

She hadn't.

I called up to the firefighters to confirm that the man in front of me was the only patient, and they confirmed, again, that they had searched the area. I knelt back down, finished hooking up the monitor, and I printed the lack of a rhythm from the cardiac monitor to take with me for my report. Standing to take another close look at my patient, I heard moaning again.

The hair on the back of my neck stood up, and I no longer ignored my intuition.

There were two things I knew at this point. The first was that my initial patient was truly dead—not-coming-back dead—and definitely not the one moaning. The second was that we were not the only ones in that forest.

I shouted up at the fire crew and my partner to search the forest again. I remembered my first impression of the scene. The area looked like a yard sale, with belongings and equipment all over the forest floor from the vehicle rolling and flinging it all out the windows and windshield.

The firefighters grumbled but reluctantly hiked down the embankment to do as I asked. After a short search, my partner found the second young man about ten feet away from us, lodged between two trees. Since it was nighttime, and he lay farther in the shadow of the trees, he was easily missed. We switched our attention to the second young man, about the same age as the first. He was unconscious and unresponsive but still alive.

As a precautionary measure, I asked the firefighters to keep searching the area. This time there was no grumbling or hesitation. My partner and I brought the man out of the forest and loaded him into the ambulance to start treatment and transport right away. We ran emergent to the closest hospital in Frisco, Colorado, and transferred care to the ER physician on duty. I checked back in on him in the morning and learned that he had lived through the night and had been transferred to a Level I Trauma Center in Denver.

I thought about that night for months afterward. What had happened in the forest? Had he been conscious enough to try to tell us he was there and where to find him? No, that couldn't be. The second patient had been completely unresponsive—meaning he did not respond to voice stimuli or pain. He was not moaning when we found him and most likely never moaned while we were there. But it was because of the moaning that I had felt uncomfortable about leaving the scene and why I asked for another search of the area. Without the moaning, we never would have seen the man, and he would have died that night in the forest due to hypothermia if not from his injuries.

The other explanation that ran through my mind was that I had been guided by something else to make sure that we did not inadvertently leave a living man to die from the elements, hidden between two trees in the forest. This was one of many times as a paramedic where following my intuition helped me make a decision that helped someone. Over time, I was able to trust those feelings more, and I began listening to the inner voice regularly.

Even today, every time I drive by that stretch of road on Hoosier Pass, I feel a presence in the forest. Even if I am distracted, I will pause and look through the trees to see if I can make out something or someone. I am certain that something is there. I don't know if it is just the memory of the night that attracts me or the spirit of the young man who died, but I have been drawn back to that spot on more than one occasion. I hope that the young man has now moved on and is not still lingering in the forest. The thought of that brings me great sadness. So, now, every time I pass, I send up a message asking him to move on in the hope that if he is there, he will hear me and try to go home.

Do you believe in the unknown?

When I was a child, I locked myself out of our family's house in Parker, Colorado. We never locked our doors out in the country, so I didn't have a key, and I knew my parents didn't carry one either. I was scared that my dad would get mad at me for getting locked out of the house, and I panicked a bit. I ran around the house, checking every door and window, but nothing would budge. Knowing my parents wouldn't be home for several hours, I knew I was stuck hanging out outside until someone came home.

To make matters worse, it started to rain.

Then came the hail.

Crying, frantic, I pulled and pulled on the glass door, hoping to get inside before the lightning and hail intensified. As a last effort, before completely giving up, I leaned back, tilted my head to the sky, and shouted to the universe, "I just need some help!"

Feeling hopeless, I took one last chance and grabbed the handle of the door to yank at it again. This time, the door glided easily open as if it had never been locked in the first place.

This was the first time in my memory that something extraordinary happened that could not be easily explained. I had tried that door at least one hundred times before finally asking for help and having the door easily open.

All of us experience the joy of birth and the sadness of death. These things are a normal part of every life. But few allow themselves the experience of the unknown. The in-between. As a paramedic,

I did find a few of those people—I think that empathic people are drawn to the professions of helpers. It was even common to hear a medic yell, "Get back in your body!" when shocking a cardiac arrest patient, knowing that if the spirit was nearby, it might need specific instructions for a good outcome.

One paramedic I worked with told me that following the death of a patient in the ambulance, the paramedic could see the spirit of the patient sitting next to her on the bench seat. Another paramedic told me that he had been working in the ER of a local hospital when a patient arrested. He went into the room to help work on the patient. The hospital staff and the paramedic were able to get the patient back after several minutes of CPR, drug therapy, and shocking the patient. When he spoke to the patient later, she said that she was able to see everything going on in the room as her spirit hovered in the corner of the room over the hospital staff as they worked to save her. She even described each person who had come to help—information she could not have known otherwise.

I learned early on in my career that decisions are made just as often because of a gut instinct as they are for known medical reasons. I heard emergency services workers state again and again, "I don't know, something just doesn't feel right," just before a patient went sideways or a scene turned out to be dangerous.

One of the most profound lessons I learned as a paramedic was to listen to my gut and to always follow my instincts. No matter the situation, this lesson has provided the right path. It took having a career rooted in science to understand that science cannot explain everything. Throughout my career as a medic, my belief in the unknown became much more pronounced, and instead of just hearing other people's stories, I experienced many unusual occurrences of my own. At first, they were scary, then they were confusing, but in time I learned that our innate intuition is one of our greatest gifts. Each one of us should work to harness that gift and use it in our daily lives. Who knows, perhaps we will see miracles happen.

Do you believe in the unknown?
I didn't always, but I do now.

PHASE 2:
LEARNING

When life itself seems lunatic, who knows where madness lies? Perhaps to be too practical is madness. To surrender dreams—this may be madness. Too much sanity may be madness—and maddest of all: to see life as it is, and not as it should be.

—Miguel De Cervantes Saavedra, *Don Quixote*

CHAPTER 4

First, Do No Harm

On a cold winter night, while still a rookie EMT, my partner and I were called to an automobile accident in the river near Breckenridge. My adrenaline skyrocketed, amped at the thought of saving someone from the frigid river. When my paramedic partner and I arrived on scene, we were told that the driver and passengers had been taken to a nearby home for warmth. We quickly drove to the house and parked in the driveway. My partner told me to grab the medical bag and other equipment and meet him inside. I hurried to the back of the ambulance and grabbed all I could think we would need. I slung the medical bag over my shoulder and sprinted from the ambulance to the house. I was excited; this had the potential to be a great call. Adrenaline swam in my system, just waiting to make me do something stupid.

My partner had gone through a sliding glass door into the living room of the home, so I quickly headed in that direction, not wanting to miss anything. Unbeknownst to me, the door had a bit of a lip at the bottom, so instead of being the hero that saved the day, I ended up tripping on that lip and sailing into the room headfirst. The firefighters, my partner, and even the patients ducked as my stethoscope, IV supplies, and the medical bag flew into the room at high speed. I, on the other hand, skidded into the room on my face, sprawled out on the floor.

The patients were fighting hypothermia, so after the abrupt entry, they immediately disregarded my presence. I obviously was not the one in control here. The firefighters worked to hide their laughter as they continued assisting with patient care. My partner's head was down as he gathered patient vitals, but his eyes slowly traveled up to my face on the floor before shaking his head in contempt. From that point forward, he completely disregarded my presence, much like the others.

Humiliated and trying to pull myself together, I jumped up and began collecting all the equipment from throughout the room. I asked if I could help with anything, but my partner and the firefighters ignored me. So instead of getting to be a part of a great call, I ended up being the butt of everyone's jokes for weeks following. I hadn't yet learned the three primary rules of EMS: first, do no harm. The second and third rules are: no running and no yelling. No matter how bad the call, there is never a reason to run into a scene. If you allow adrenaline to guide your actions, mistakes will be made, and people will suffer.

My guides have an extremely sick sense of humor and take their teaching responsibilities seriously. Becoming the laughingstock of the ambulance service was an excellent motivator to do better. Point taken. Lesson learned.

EARLY IN MY career, I worked closely with a paramedic named Bob. He was one of my field training instructors when I was a brand-new EMT, and later, he was an instructor after completing paramedic school. Bob was a unique paramedic and individual. I have not met another soul like him on this earth. To say he was methodical is an understatement. He was deliberate in everything he did. What I liked most about him, however, was that he knew he was not like anyone else but never let it change him. He didn't try to be someone he wasn't and was extremely comfortable in his own skin.

Now, I tend to move pretty fast. I always have. My thoughts race 100 mph, and I talk equally fast. So, working with Bob could sometimes be a challenge. Where I was fast, Bob was slow. When we would get a call, I'd run to the ambulance and wait while Bob slowly finished his tea.

"Come on, Bob, let's go. We have a call."

"I'll meet you in the ambulance," he'd reply, not moving.

Slowly, he would then get up and walk, as if on a Sunday stroll, to the ambulance. I'd be ready in the passenger seat before Bob even hit the stairs to go down to the ambulance bay. He'd open the driver's side door, sit down, make sure his lunch was stored away properly, look over to ensure my seatbelt was fastened before fastening his own, and then—only then—would he start the ambulance and drive to the call. The whole time, I wanted to shake my hands in the air and scream, "Let's go, already!"

Bob drove me crazy! The adrenaline flowed in my rookie veins, and I wanted to save lives, dammit! I was willing to break all speeding records to get to my unfortunate victim. The only thing getting in my way was Bob.

It was after the incident at the river where I'd thoroughly humiliated myself that I took a good long look at Bob's way of doing things. Yes, he moved slower than molasses and talked as if he just took a bong hit, but maybe there was a reason for it all. After my experience of tripping and flying head-first into an emergency scene, I started to watch Bob more closely, and I ended up learning so much more than what he had to teach me in paramedicine. *No running and no yelling* became my mantra. I learned to live by it. I cannot say I was ever as slow as Bob (no one could ever be as slow as Bob), but I did take more time. I walked calmly to emergency scenes and noticed how much a calm demeanor calmed others. By showing fear or being out of control, you can—and will—make scenes much worse for those working them or for the families watching. It can effectively break the first rule of EMS, "First, do no harm."

What I have noticed time and again is that when I get stressed, the people around me get stressed as well. If I raise my voice, I can physically feel the tension in the room increase. And when people are tense, they don't think clearly and don't react appropriately.

I picked a stressful profession. As a paramedic and firefighter, lives were literally in my hands every time I went out on a call. And as an emergency manager, entire communities depend upon my expertise to get them through one of their darkest days. Stress comes with these jobs—but in many ways, it is good stress. It is a calling to help when needed.

To this day, I think of Bob every time I enter an emergency operations center. Inside, I may feel the butterflies in my stomach or the impending dread of what might happen, but on the outside, I do my best to breathe and walk slowly, smile, and try to calm the room. I am not always successful, but in those times that I am, I witness how a room can turn from chaos to a well-oiled machine with everyone doing their part to respond to the disaster and make life a little easier for those most impacted.

Bob taught me many things over the years, but his greatest lesson has been a lasting one, and one he probably never meant to teach me. Bob taught me to take a bit more time, take a deep breath, look around, feel the room, and perhaps, make everything just a little better just by being present.

Thank you, Bob.

CHAPTER 5

WATCHING

"WHAT ON EARTH are you doing?" I asked the firefighters. "We are trying to get the patient restrained, but she is being . . . (grunt) . . . difficult."

I glanced at the gurney as the firefighters worked to get it into the back of the ambulance. The patient had grabbed onto both open doors and spread her legs in an effort to jam herself in the doorway, making it impossible to get her inside the ambulance to begin transport.

She had left her condo quietly on the gurney only to become combative by the time we reached the parked ambulance. It was 3 a.m. and our third difficult call since midnight.

After several minutes and the help of four firefighters, my partner and I had restrained the patient so that she couldn't cause harm to herself or anyone else during the trip to the hospital. Since she was so combative, I asked a firefighter, Emily, to drive the ambulance so that my partner and I could remain in the back with the patient.

Once we were ready to go, I looked through the opening in the ambulance from the patient compartment to the driver's seat and gave Emily a thumbs up. She took her foot off the brake and started forward. After about five feet, the ambulance came to an abrupt stop with a crash. My partner skidded across the bench seat, hitting his head on the cabinets near the side door, while I held on to the grab bar in the jump seat.

I whipped around to talk through the compartment between the back of the ambulance and the driver's seat.

"What's wrong?"

Emily turned to face me. "I think I hit the balcony of one of these units."

As she told me this, a loud air horn pierced through the quiet night. Not long after, lights came on in condos around the area as people woke from the noise.

Irritated, Emily swung around and unrolled her window to yell at the fire crew. "I know I hit the building. Stop honking the horn!"

Emily turned again to face me, firmly anchoring her left foot on the floor, when we heard the air horn sound one more time. She quickly whipped back around and yelled again to "stop honking the air horn!" The fire crew held their hands up in the air, with confused expressions on their faces.

I thought Emily was going to kill her crew.

Realizing what was happening, I leaned in toward Emily in the driver's seat.

"Emily," I said through the passageway to the driver's compartment, "It isn't your crew honking at you. Every time you turn to talk to us, you are hitting the button on the floor for the air horn."

Emily looked down at the floor near her left foot to see the round silver knob sticking out of the floor and then looked up toward the ceiling and closed her eyes briefly, clearly mortified. Not only had she hit someone's balcony, but she had also woken up the entire neighborhood to witness the accident by both honking the horn and yelling at her crew, completely confusing the firefighters in the engine who were quietly waiting.

By this time, dozens of people were at their front doors or standing at their windows watching the drama unfold.

TUNNEL VISION IS a bitch.

As I learned to slow my pace, I also became a watcher. I watched my coworkers as they attended to patients, I watched hospital staff, and I watched each scene to learn more about human nature. While in paramedic school, one of my preceptors would not let me go near the patient on any scene and she insisted that I give direction from the doorway for all activities. After so much time as an EMT working directly with a patient, this was a difficult task for me. But I quickly realized that the reason she wanted me to direct patient care from the door was so I would have a full view of everything going on around me. I could better see a pending threat or perhaps the answer to a question about the patient's condition. There would be less chance of tunnel vision if I stepped back to see everything on the scene. I later noticed that our physician adviser would sit in a chair in the corner of the room whenever we brought in a serious patient. The more serious the injuries or illness, the farther away he sat. He, too, wanted to ensure he could see everything going on in the room instead of getting too close and losing perspective.

When I was young, I could have been classified as an extrovert. If I liked a song, I'd jump up on a table and start to dance. Once I jumped on stage at Elitch Gardens and sang along as the band performed '50s hits. I had a level of confidence around others that allowed me to do anything that came to mind without thinking about the consequences.

Once I became a paramedic, I changed. I became more cautious, and I became a watcher. I learned to stand apart from the scene and analyze it as a whole instead of as an individual part. I looked, and I listened to all around me. I watched crowds and human behavior.

I also developed an increased awareness of those around me, leading to strong empathic abilities. For a long time I thought it started with a better understanding of body language and facial expressions that I believed came from my tendency to watch people closely. But as I learned more about how the brain works and how trauma creates behaviors, I know that the reason I pay such close attention to body language and the reason I watched people so closely was because childhood trauma had taught me to watch out for the bottom to drop out. When living in an alcoholic's home, the rest of the family becomes hypervigilant, paying attention to each and every cue so that we can be prepared for what might happen. This, in turn led to empathic abilities and a strong intuition that grew while working as a paramedic.

Most of my empathic abilities come from my stomach. I feel all the emotions around me. Some call this clairsentience—the ability to sense what is going on. Think of it as a superpowered gut feeling. I can pass someone in the grocery store and feel everything they are feeling. On more than one occasion, I have passed someone and been suddenly angry for no reason, only to realize later that the emotions were not my own. This, too, has led me to pull away from people in my life. There's only so much emotion one person can absorb without needing to get away from it all.

Being alone allows me to recharge and balance my energy. But it has also caused a level of isolation I haven't since been able to shake. Somewhere in this process, I ended up standing apart from everyone around me. I stopped letting people in.

I have learned that this is common for those who are empathic. We are the ones in the room who cannot wait to get the chance to leave and go home. We are the ones who read, garden, contemplate, and go to the movies without the need to have someone join us. But we also love those close friendships and relationships where you find that one person that you can talk to for hours about everything the universe has to offer. We are the watchers and the seekers who know we don't know everything.

When I worked as a field manager for the State of Colorado, I would arrive at a local emergency operations center and the first thing

I would do was stop at the door, take a deep breath, and walk slowly into the room. I'd look around at all the faces and the activity to get a quick picture of all that was going on before I sat down and got to work. The emergency manager was often incredibly busy and stressed by the time I arrived, so having a broad picture allowed me to assist them in a calm and controlled manner, bringing some type of order to the chaos. I loved this part of my job, and it was only because of my work as a medic and my strengthening empathic abilities that I learned it so well.

Paramedicine transformed me from a social creature with many friends and always an activity to attend to a student of human behavior. Paramedicine taught me to slow down and look around. In the words of Ferris Bueller, "Life moves pretty fast. If you don't stop and look around once in a while, you could miss it." I learned to see a world of unimaginable beauty, even in the midst of trauma.

CHAPTER 6

Invisibility

I JUMPED OUT of the ambulance, looked up, and stopped in my tracks. Nothing but desert, hills, and sagebrush for as far as I could see. I was at the end of my clinical rotation in Boulder, and the crew had driven to the outskirts of town for our next call.

"Where are we?" I asked.

"Psych call. We were told a man was out here."

Our ambulance arrived on scene to find . . . nothing. The terrain was dry, with few trees, lots of sagebrush, and hard-packed dirt. Only the police cruiser parked in front of us announced that we were in the right place. As I opened the side door and stepped out of the ambulance into the bright light of summer with the medical bag, a tall forty-year-old man came stomping over the hill straight toward us, kicking up a cloud of dust all around him.

"That's it," he shouted. "The wedding is off!"

I looked around the scene again, but there was truly nothing out there but dirt, rocks, and sagebrush—not a single person outside of emergency responders and this lone man. He was clearly agitated, pacing in front of us, flinging his arms in the air and pointing at us accusingly.

"You have ruined everything! You can't just drive through a wedding."

The officer tried to get him to stop pacing and talk to us. "Sir, we had a report of someone in distress here. Do you mind talking with us for a minute?"

"You don't understand," he said, truly distressed. "The lizard will never come now. You have to leave."

Hmmm. Okay.

Through the course of our conversation, we pieced together that a giant lizard was supposed to come up over the hill once everyone was in place, and he was to officiate the wedding. The man described an elaborate setup with hundreds of people all around us, waiting and angry because we had disturbed the proceedings.

I had never been on a call with a patient who described seeing things I could not see where the patient was so earnest and believable. He seemed absolutely normal, knew who he was, where he was, and apparently why he was there. The longer I spoke with him, the more I wondered about the scene. Maybe *we* were the crazy ones, and there actually were hundreds of people all staring at us, waiting for us to leave so that the lizard could finally wed the couple.

After talking with him for a while, we finally convinced him to go in and get a medical evaluation. If all went well, he could return to the wedding for what sounded like a memorable reception.

As part of my ill-conceived "fearless forties," I decided I would tackle that which had kept me bound in the past. In 2011, as part of this crusade, I decided to take a leap and go on a singles cruise for my fortieth birthday. I had never been on a cruise before and had never been to the Caribbean. One of my goals was to open up and meet new people. I found a singles cruise that would travel for seven days and nights to several tropical locations, and in the meantime, the cruise would have multiple activities for the five hundred single people on the ship. Perfect. I planned the trip, paid for everything, and flew down to Florida to start my adventure.

The minute I arrived in my hotel room, however, my original fears came flooding back. Are those black spots before my eyes? Am I going to faint? What the hell am I doing in Florida getting ready to board a singles cruise? I was about to be trapped on a boat with a bunch of other single people. I don't drink. I hate small talk. I don't even really like people. Visions of a meat market on water with no way to escape slammed into my brain.

Breath quickening.

Heart racing.

This was going to be a disaster!

I decided to skip the "lock and key" party where all the women have a lock, and the men have a key, and you have to find the person with the key that matches your lock. Instead, I curled up into the fetal position on my hotel bed and dreaded the next day.

When I woke, I remembered that I had just turned forty, and this was supposed to be my fearless forties, so I gave myself a pep talk, told myself to stop being a whiny little bitch, walked to the ship, and got onboard.

My first cruise. It would be okay.

The first night aboard, we were assigned seats for everyone in the dining hall. I sat with seven other people at a large round table and had a nice dinner. I even met a guy at the table who was funny and kind. We started talking about books and philosophy, and as the night wore on, the conversation came more easily between us.

The woman sitting right next to me drank quite a lot during dinner (and most likely before), and by dessert, she was well and truly hammered. Toward the end of dinner, she leaned closer to me and expressed loudly, "You two are really hitting it off; you should go for it." Her words slurred and, in true drunk fashion, she went on and on about my new friend and me hooking up.

All the uneasiness and fear returned. I felt the heat on my face. I am Irish, so my face goes from pale white to bright red in a matter of seconds when I am uncomfortable. I looked across the table and smiled apologetically at the man with whom I had conversed. He looked just as uncomfortable as I felt, and right before my eyes, I witnessed him shutting down and closing off any further conversation. And yet, the drunk woman to my left would not stop talking.

By this time in my life, I had developed a truly low tolerance level for intoxicated people. Sure, you want to go out and have a few drinks, by all means. But without fail, drunks can identify me in a crowded room. Then they latch themselves onto me and never leave. It is like the German shepherd who finds the one person in the room who feels uncomfortable around dogs, so the big hulking beast runs straight up to that person and licks them in the face and puts his nose in their crotch.

Knowing that the evening had gone quickly to hell, I finally turned to my drunk friend and said, "Would you mind shutting the fuck up?" Then I stood, put my napkin down, left the table and went back to the comfort and safety of my room.

The next morning, vowing to start anew, I ventured out on the ship to see what activities might be awaiting me. As I wandered through the halls, one of the men that was sitting at our table from the night before passed by me and then stopped me.

"You're Lori, right?" he asked.

I smiled. "Yes, we met last night at dinner."

"Have you seen the other Laurie?" he asked excitedly. "You know, the one with the big . . . you know . . .?" He held his hands in front of his chest, indicating a well-endowed woman.

Seriously!

"Umm, no. I have not seen her."

Crestfallen, his smile disappeared. "Oh, okay. Thanks." And he walked out of my life forever.

That's it! No more!

I decided at that moment that this was *my* vacation, and I would make the most of it by myself. To hell with all these assholes. And I am happy to report that I did have a wonderful time. I found the Serenity Deck—it is just as it is named—and I lay in a hammock and read my book. I went swimming, I found the spa, and I explored each of our destinations thoroughly. Surprisingly, I also met a great group of people with whom I met up at the end of each day for dinner.

Throughout most of my life, I have felt invisible. I can be in a room of people, and it doesn't seem that anyone even knows I am there. I have spoken directly to someone while making eye contact, and they hear nothing and look past me. It is an interesting phenomenon.

In high school, I had a mad crush on my longtime friend Tommy. I thought he was just dreamy. We hung out together and went to parties, and I thought he was *the one*. But in all those years, I was only ever seen as a friend. In later years, this happened time and time again. I was not seen as someone to love, and on more than one occasion, a guy I really liked admitted to me that he had always thought I was a lesbian.

Perfect! My ability to woo was extraordinary.

As a watcher, being invisible can be a great strength. I can sit back and watch interactions without anyone getting upset or thinking I am intruding. I can study human behavior and learn from those around me. It has also given me the great ability to hone my intuition and to see things that others don't.

Remember the lizard guy? The patient who was upset that I messed up his wedding. By the time he had told me his story, I was half convinced that all those people were actually there and that my limited mind just couldn't see them. He was so convincing because he truly saw everything he told us about. I kept glancing around, thinking that everyone would suddenly appear like the ball players in *Field of Dreams*. Maybe there was nothing wrong with the man's mind at all, and it was the rest of us that just weren't open enough to see the full picture. He had chosen the red pill and had entered the Matrix while the rest of us remained blissfully unaware.

As a watcher, psych patients provided an entirely new level of experience. How do we know that what they see or hear isn't real? In some cases, it was obviously best for everyone to bring the patient in and have them evaluated. For others, I watched and listened and could almost believe that a giant iguana was about to come up over the hill.

The interactions I have had with the unknown tell me that I am not alone. The spirit world has never treated me as if I am invisible. Since my first foray into developing my intuition and discovering the spirit world, my spirit guides have shown me that they see me and know I am here. They follow my movements wherever I go and ensure that I understand that I am never alone. In times of great stress or anxiety, these guides show up and make their presence known, whether it is the movement of a pan on the stove from one burner to the next, the flickering of lights in the house, or abrupt clapping or whistling in my ears to get my attention. Each action is meant to remind me that while I often feel alone in the human world, I am not alone in the greater universe.

There is so much we do not understand about our world and our existence. But what I have come to know over the years is that each of us was brought here for a purpose and that it is up to each of us to figure this out and learn the lessons we are meant to learn. None of us is invisible, and none of us is alone. Some of us just must depend on the unknown.

And if it means I never have to talk to the guy looking for the Laurie with the big . . . you know . . . well, then I am good.

CHAPTER 7

Fear

I SPENT MANY years as a volunteer firefighter for the Snake River Fire Protection District in Summit County, Colorado. From 1998 to 2001, I also lived in the fire station in the small town of Montezuma as a resident firefighter. Those of us who lived in the fire stations took care of the equipment, cleaned the space, and ran calls after hours. In Montezuma, there was a one-bay fire station. Attached was a two-bedroom apartment where I lived with my roommate, Julian.

As my empathic abilities began to grow, I grew more curious about what was going on. I didn't have a lot of knowledge at this time about anything but science, but I knew enough to know something had changed, and I wanted to know more. I began reading books about intuition and spirituality to try to gain a deeper understanding of the world around me. And much like my early years as an EMT, I made some rookie mistakes.

If there was something out there, some unknown force guiding my path, I wanted to let it in. And, as with most things, my impatience got the best of me. While reading a book on spirits, I decided to tell the universe that I was ready. I was open and willing to receive.

Shortly thereafter, while asleep at the firehouse, I woke up with a start. I sat straight up, gasping for breath, wondering what had awakened me so suddenly. As I cleared my eyes, I realized I was not alone in the room. I slept in a twin bed against the wall in a small bedroom on the second floor of the two-bedroom apartment attached to the fire station. Julian worked nights, so he was not in his room down the hall. As I tried to get my lungs to work, I recognized that a man was sitting at the end of my bed watching me. Not a flesh-and-blood man, but an entity. Yup, that is what I said—an entity. Not of this earth. An apparition. A spirit. Whatever you wish to call it.

I felt a heaviness, a darkness. I heard him breathing and felt him sitting next to my legs. I could even see the indent on the bed where he sat. He stared right into my eyes.

I felt trapped.

I also could not seem to get my lungs to work. It was as if I'd had the wind knocked out of me, and my lungs had seized. All I could do was sit there and stare at him as he stared back. He seemed either angry or extremely unhappy, and I could not tell if the anger was directed at me. As for what he looked like, there was darkness—a hazy grayish-black energy. I thought he looked like a demon—a force of evil. And I had invited him in.

Nothing like this had ever happened to me before, and even though I had been reading about expanding my intuition, I obviously was ill-prepared for this event. I also would not have said I believed in something like an evil entity or a demon prior to this experience. Absolutely paralyzed with fear, I sat there for several minutes, unable to function.

I finally snapped out of it and took in a great big gasp of air. Everything started working again. I quickly flung my legs off the bed and ran out of the room and out of the house. I even left my dog behind, I was so scared (I still feel bad about that—sorry, Mystic).

I worked at Keystone Resort, so I went to my office and spent the rest of the night on the floor of my office until my shift began in the morning. Later that afternoon, while on shift, my EMT partner and

I received a call in River Run regarding a woman who had suffered a mental breakdown. We were called to a woman at a restaurant who had given her underwear to the waiter as he took her order.

"You take this," my paramedic partner said. "You are always good with psych patients."

He was right. Historically, I did well with some of the more fragile patients or those close to breaking down. I was generally good with people suffering from psychiatric trauma, so I agreed to lead the call.

I approached the woman alone, walking slowly, to try to calm her and talk to her, but the moment she saw me, she totally flipped. She reeled back with horror at my presence and pointed just above my right ear. Worse, she began to describe the man I had seen at the end of my bed at the firehouse just hours earlier. According to her, the man was with me, hovering over my shoulder with his dark energy. She described him as dressed all in black and extremely angry.

The hair on the back of my neck stood up, and a deep fear crept into my body. For a moment, I froze again, as if I were back in my small bedroom staring at the man sitting next to me. I kept it together long enough to get our patient to the hospital for treatment, and then I returned home to get my dog because I just couldn't stay there alone any longer. With the new knowledge that the darkness had possibly followed me from home, I was unable to sleep or eat and remained in a constant state of fear.

After a few days, I knew I had to do something. I took a day off, went down to Denver, and decided to go to a metaphysical bookstore to grab some reading material and try to figure everything out. This was prior to computers and the Internet, so I did what I knew. I sought out books that might explain what had happened and what I might do about the darkness that had decided we were besties.

I had never been to this store before. It was a small shop on a busy street filled with books, incense, tarot cards, candles, and other spiritual items. As I entered, the woman behind the counter took one look at me and said, "You need to go back."

I stopped abruptly, looked behind me and around me, but I was the only person in the store with her. She had a sad smile on her face as she continued to look directly at me.

Stepping forward, I asked, "What do you mean?"

"You need to go back. You cannot let the spirits have that kind of control over you. Go home and make sure they know the rules of your house."

This information was provided to me before I ever said a word about what had happened in the firehouse. I had never been there before. I broke down into tears as she slowly talked to me about how important boundaries are when working with spirits. She explained that I needed to lay down the rules, and she gave me some ideas for how to protect myself in the future. I was too much in shock to ask all the questions I had, so I just took what I heard and returned home.

When I entered my room, I noticed that a large picture that had been on my wall was lying in the middle of the room, smashed into several pieces. This almost kept me from doing what I knew I needed to do. The fear quickly returned, and I noticed my hands shaking. I took a seat on the ground with my back against my bed and spoke out loud to the empty room.

"I don't know who you are or what you want," I started, "but this is my house, and you are not welcome here if you mean to cause harm."

I set the boundaries I was taught to set and stayed in the room until the fear finally subsided. From that day forward, I was comfortable enough in the firehouse to live and sleep there, but I never felt completely at ease. Also, my dog started to act strange. Whenever I closed the closet door in the hallway, she would bark at it wildly, but once opened, she'd sit on her hind legs and watch the inside of the closet calmly as if watching a movie. Dogs are supposed to be a comfort, but this was just plain creepy.

For a few years following this event, I felt a presence with me wherever I went. I felt what the woman in River Run had seen—some type of dark energy behind me, following me. He never made himself known again, but I felt him, nonetheless. I finally returned to the same metaphysical bookstore to ask some questions. After my first experience, I knew that the woman behind the counter was the real deal, so I felt I could trust what she had to say. Interestingly, she did not feel that the spirit was evil. She agreed that he was with me, but she stressed that what I felt in the darkness was pain, not evil. He had burned in a saloon fire many years earlier, and he stayed with me because I was the first person who saw him and felt his presence.

After that, I did not fear his presence and got somewhat used to him being around. After a while, I no longer felt him with me. Perhaps he finally moved on or found some peace. I did do some research on the firehouse, though, and found that it was built on land where a saloon once stood. That saloon burned down in the late 1800s.

THE FIRST TIME I felt fear was the first time I heard thunder. In Eastern Colorado, the thunder can shake your entire house. Windows rattle and the vibration of the enormous sound can make your heart skip a beat. I thought the world was crashing in around me. I ran into my parents' bedroom screaming. Once awake, my parents calmed me and told me that thunder was the noise that was made when clouds crashed into one another and that the lightning was the spark from the crash. This made perfect sense to my two- or three-year-old brain. Nothing to fear there—just a bit of weather.

I had a normal early childhood, for the most part. Both parents were kind and funny and giving. But as I grew, things began to change. By the time I finished elementary school and entered junior high, a more persistent fear took hold—one that still leaves its mark today. Alcoholism and drug addiction had entered our home.

Life became unpredictable. Sometimes we had money, and other times I felt the strain of my family just getting by. My fun-loving father, who I loved to spend time with as a little girl, turned into a moody and erratic stranger. I hated when the police would arrive at our house late at night, knocking on our door. My brothers and I would look at one another, not knowing if we should open the door. I didn't know if they were there to take my father away or to tell us that my father would never be coming home. We all hesitated each time but ultimately opened the door to talk with them.

I also never knew what condition my father would be in once he did get home. On several occasions he came home bruised and bloody from a fight at the bar. Once I found him sitting at the kitchen table eating leftovers from the fridge with a large gash across his forehead and eyebrow. He explained that someone had thrown a Chinese star at his head. He said it with pride while explaining how he'd ultimately won that fight.

The smallest things suddenly set off my father's anger. It got so bad that by middle school, my brothers and I would hide downstairs in the basement when we heard his car on the driveway because we didn't know if it was Good Dad or Bad Dad returning home. His boots had a distinctive sound on the floor upstairs, and when we heard them hit the floor, fear was always my first reaction. Sometimes my dad came home, grabbed some food, and quietly went to bed. Other times, we heard him in the kitchen slamming cabinet doors or muttering under his breath before finally walking to the top of the stairs and yelling down at the three of us to come upstairs. This was when I was most anxious as a child. Not knowing as I walked up the stairs what I would find but knowing I could not ignore his order.

One night, I woke to the smell of fish. As I cleared my head, I felt fish hitting my face and body. My father stood angrily at my bedroom door, hurling pieces of fish at me.

"Who the fuck left the fish on the counter?" he screamed.

I was too confused to fully understand what was going on, so I just hid my head under the covers and waited for him to leave. "I'm sorry," I said, over and over. More likely than not, he was the one who'd taken the fish out of the freezer only to forget about it a few minutes later, but that didn't matter. I learned to just freeze and wait for his wrath to end, his fury to dissipate. If I engaged or asked a question, his anger rose again, and I just prolonged the incident.

This became a new norm in my teenage years. My father became more unpredictable, and I mastered the flight and freeze trauma responses. I would either flee the minute I felt conflict, or I would freeze and try to be as invisible as possible until the threat passed.

This time in my life also led to other fears—fear of failure, fear of the unknown, fear of closeness, and fear of the bottom falling out. My dad had been my hero when I was a young girl. He was an amazing artist who drew these elaborate pictures for me. He also had a sharp mind. He could solve any math problem you gave him in his head. Mostly, he was so much fun! We had food fights, we sang together, we both loved watching horror movies late into the night, and he generously gave of himself.

Unfortunately, every one of those traits had its opposite in my alcoholic father. He no longer did anything with us kids and was gone at the bar much of the time. Everything that was once fun had turned sour, and instead of waiting impatiently for him to come home at the end of the day, I dreaded his return. It was just too much change in too little time in my young life to keep up.

By high school, I had mastered the ability to keep my home life private from my friends and I retreated into social activities whenever I could so that I would be away from the unpredictability of home. It wasn't until my junior year that the two lives collided.

I woke to the phone ringing. I looked up and realized I had slept in and missed the school bus. We were a week away from the state championships and I had also missed band practice that morning. I flung the covers off my bed and answered the phone.

"Hello."

"Where the fuck are you?" my band director yelled into the phone.

I ran a hand through my hair and rubbed my face. I didn't know what to say, so I just said, "I'm sorry, I had a really bad night."

"I don't give a fuck what kind of night you had. Never miss practice again!"

Before I could say anything more, he slammed down the phone, hanging up.

My heart raced. I had never had a teacher speak to me like that, with such anger. I felt as if I had let everyone down. I quickly dressed and grabbed my book bag before heading upstairs. Without a car of my own, and no one else home, I was forced to wake my sleeping father and ask him to drive me to school. He absolutely hated being woken up, so my day was about to get much worse.

I tentatively walked into his room and approached the bed, gently shaking him.

"Dad?"

After a few tries he finally opened his eyes. "What do you want?"

"I need a ride to school." I said softly, standing by the door. "I missed the bus."

After getting my second tongue lashing of the morning, he finally got up and got dressed. Shortly after that he learned that my brother had taken his car without his permission. My father's dark mood grew before my eyes. When he became really angry, he'd get quiet. This is when I feared him the most.

We both got into a second car my dad had in the driveway and he drove me to school. Upon entering the parking lot, we both saw my brother get out of the car he'd taken without permission. My father slammed the vehicle into park and stormed out of the car, already yelling at my brother. Kent was a senior that year and he and my father regularly argued. This time, my father was in a blind rage and he and my brother started fighting in the school parking lot. My father kept hitting Kent over and over while I sat in the passenger seat of the car just screaming for them to stop.

My father knocked my brother onto the hood of another vehicle and screamed, "I am going to break every bone in your body!"

It wasn't until this point that I looked around and saw the number of people that were watching the fight unfold. For the first time, my friends and teachers were all witness to my father's rage. I could no longer just shrink and disappear into myself. Instead, I would be forced to confront everything over and over again throughout the day as I encountered students, faculty and staff.

I could no longer pretend everything was normal.

Once fear crept in, it was impossible to completely remove. I couldn't go back to the time when I felt no fear and I knew I could count on my father when I needed him most. Instead, I built up mechanisms of protection. I stepped away from my father and locked him out of the things that went on in my life.

Unfortunately, this also caused me to retreat from my mother, who had always been supportive and kind and worked as a buffer between us kids and our father. I stayed away from home as much as possible, hanging out with my friends or going to the movies by myself. This is probably the beginning of my independent streak, which has lasted a lifetime. It was also the beginning of a long list of coping mechanisms to try to handle my new fears.

I was born in 1971, right in the middle of the Gen X years. I have always loved being Gen X—it is the one place where I fit the mold perfectly. I was a latchkey child, leading to a fierce independent streak as well as the ability to critically think through my problems to find solutions. The X in Generation X stands for those who wish not to be defined, those who plow their own path. On the downside, our generation has also grown up with attachment issues and the certainty that things just won't work out. We wait for the bottom to fall out.

So, am I a product of my generation or my upbringing in a home with an abusive alcoholic? I am not certain, but I do know that all these characteristics come from the ability of the body and mind to recover from trauma and build up mechanisms to survive and thrive. I learned not to sit in the basement trembling in fear and waiting for the bottom to drop out—I started to prepare for it, knowing that one day it would come.

Hello amygdala!

My first real brush with my own death at the age of forty-three, sitting in the ER desperately trying to breathe, created a new unknown, and a new bottom that might fall out. Instead of being wary of individuals around me, I was wary of my own body and what it tried to tell me each day. I had been healthy prior to turning forty, so these fears about my health were a new and extremely unwelcome experience.

Three years later, I ended up in the emergency room again. This time I woke at 5 a.m. with excruciating stomach pain. Again, my first thought was not to call an ambulance. Instead, I made it to my car and drove to the ER. I hadn't experienced pain like this in the past, so I had no idea what could be happening.

The pain was near my belly button and came in waves—sharp, intense pains, each one getting stronger. Doubled up in pain, unable to walk straight, I slowly moved through the automatic doors into the ER. When the staff saw me, they immediately grabbed a wheelchair and helped me to sit before taking me straight back to a room. My heart rate and blood pressure were both incredibly elevated, leading the nurses to try to coax me to breathe through my pain.

In the horrific minutes that followed, as I lay in the fetal position on the hospital bed, the nurses and doctors ran several tests and took me for an abdominal CT scan. When the results were clear, the doctor came back into my room to tell me that I needed to have emergency surgery for a ruptured duodenal ulcer, a life-threatening condition. After a seemingly endless round of tests and waiting in pain, a sudden burst of movement and activity occurred around me as I was whisked into surgery. I cannot tell you how good it felt to have the anesthesia begin to work, lessening the pain and anxiety as I drifted off to sleep.

I spent another week in the hospital and was released home attached to a feeding tube while my body recovered. Three weeks later, while having lunch with a friend, I experienced another pulmonary embolism. I knew the moment it happened this time, with a sharp pain just under my right breast with shortness of breath immediately following.

Another hospital stay for me.

And within another six months, I ended up back in the hospital with another perforated ulcer, leading to more time in the hospital and in recovery at home. Suddenly, instead of feeling healthy and strong in my forties, I felt like I was eighty years old—frail and fragile. I felt invincible as a child because I could plan for the unknown, but now, I just felt that tragedy was a heartbeat away.

I hated that feeling of fragility. I did not want to be weak. I wanted to be strong and face my fears. But I learned that we don't always get what we want, and sometimes, the lessons we are to learn come in undesirable ways.

CHAPTER 8

ADDICTION

WHILE WORKING IN the Emergency Department of a hospital in Denver as part of my clinicals to finish paramedic school, an ambulance brought a new patient into the ER. He was heavily intoxicated, belligerent, and spouting off at anyone who interacted with him—a seemingly typical call. I assisted the nurses and doctors in getting the patient transferred from the pram to the hospital gurney. It was then that I noticed the handcuff that attached the patient's arm to the pram. A police officer walked up behind me and unlocked the handcuffs from the pram before reattaching them to the railing on the hospital bed.

"Twenty-five-year-old male involved in a head-on collision with another vehicle," the paramedic began, giving her report. "The patient was found in the driver's seat of one of the vehicles, awake and alert upon arrival, bleeding from the head. We immobilized him and transferred him to the backboard for transport." The paramedic continued giving the patient's vitals and a systematic review of his injuries before officially transferring care to the hospital staff.

After getting him stabilized and calm, he eventually fell asleep. Other than a cut to his head and a few contusions, he left the accident relatively unscathed. Unfortunately, the family in the other car did not fare as well. I learned that he had been driving while under the influence when he crossed the yellow line and hit the other vehicle head-on. The collision had killed three children under the age of twelve, along with their father. The mother was the only one to survive. She remained in critical condition and was fighting for her life in surgery.

While the staff in the ER was just as upset as I was to hear this news, they did all that they could to ensure that this man lived just like they would for any other patient. I always found it interesting that the drunk driver almost always survived while others involved did not. It was as if the universe needed them to survive to fully understand the harm that had been caused.

I stood at the door to his room in the ER, watching him sleep. When a new police officer came to relieve the guard outside his door, I couldn't help but think about what would happen in the morning when this man woke, stone-cold sober, to find out that the simple act of getting behind the wheel after drinking caused the deaths of four people, three of them children. I felt utter sadness—not only for the deaths but for the life that continued with the knowledge of the terrible consequences of one action.

ONE THING EMERGENCY responders deal with on a daily basis is addiction. We respond to motor vehicle accidents involving intoxicated drivers, we respond to those who have overdosed—either accidentally or on purpose—and we respond to the ever-growing opioid addiction in our country. The majority of calls a paramedic will face in their careers will be drug or alcohol related.

When I was in junior high, my mom sat me down and told me about a time she tried smoking marijuana. It ended up being laced with PCP, which made her think her head was on fire. She banged her head against a wall to try to put the fire out. Her friends had to stop her before she knocked herself out or died. I don't know if the story my mother told me was true or if it was part of a "Don't Do Drugs" scare strategy, but I can say that it was highly effective.

In high school, I didn't belong to any one clique, but the group I spent the most time with were the Heshers—those you would picture hanging out in the smoking lounge at school (do they still have smoking lounges?) with jean jackets and big boots—basically, the long-haired freaky people. We listened mostly to '60s music and hard rock, and we all drank a lot of alcohol. Most of my friends also used drugs in high school. Pot, mushrooms, acid, and cocaine were the biggest drugs at the time in our community.

On more than one occasion, a high school friend came close to death due to alcohol or drugs. When I was sixteen, I spent a lot of time at the bowling alley in Parker hanging out with my friends. One Friday, at around 11:30 p.m., a friend ran inside, searched us out, and hurried toward us.

"Something's wrong with Larry," he said, gesturing for us to follow.

I rushed outside with a few others, turned the corner to the right, and saw Larry lying against the wall of the bowling alley on the sidewalk. Nothing was visibly wrong with him, except that he wasn't moving, and his head hung low to his chest. My first thought was that he might be crying.

Nervous, I knelt down and tried to get his attention. I placed my hand under his chin after no response and lifted his head to the light. When he looked up at me, I shuddered. My first thought was that I was staring into the face of death.

Larry's face was dark gray, and his eyes looked completely black. He faintly said, "Hi," and then put his head back down again as if he didn't have the power to hold it up anymore.

"What happened?" I asked his companions. My alarm at Larry's condition increased after seeing his ashen face. I thought perhaps he was on some new drug, but they all said he hadn't consumed anything but alcohol.

A few minutes later, Larry finally moved, leaned over, and began vomiting profusely. Once finished, a few of us worked to get him up on his feet and get him into a car. A cop drove through the parking lot and headed in our direction. It was past curfew in town, so we hurried to Chuck's car and got in before the cop passed by. We drove around for a while to make sure Larry was not left alone, and he slowly started to come around.

The next morning, I told my mom what I saw, and she told me that it sounded like alcohol poisoning and that Larry could have died. This was the first time I had seen the very real consequences of alcohol on someone I knew.

Although there were several instances in high school of friends doing too many drugs or me drinking too heavily, I really didn't see any of it as a problem to be corrected. We were young and having fun. I also hadn't yet connected my father's drinking and drug use with several generations of alcoholism in my family. Instead, I continued drinking rather heavily well into my twenties.

"Hey, Lori, we're coming to visit!"

"Seriously?"

"Yes, we are on our way right now, should be there later tonight."

My friends were calling me from Colorado letting me know they were coming to Vegas to visit. I was so excited! I hadn't seen my friends in the two years since graduation, so the thought of a large group of them coming to visit me got me pumped. And what better way to celebrate than to get on my bike and go play some pool and drink at the bar while I waited for their arrival.

The next thing I remember is waking up lying on my couch. I heard the television, and I heard a bunch of people talking and laughing. As I opened my eyes slowly, I found four of my high school friends sitting around me watching television.

"How did you get in my apartment?" I asked groggily, a bit embarrassed at being so hung over and having no memory of their arrival.

Everyone laughed. "When we got here," Shawn said, "Your door was wide open with your bike wedged half in and half out of the apartment." The others started to chime in. "Oh, and your dog was running around outside, so we grabbed her and brought her home."

I lifted my head to look around the room, finding my dog curled up in Roy's lap in the chair by the couch. Knowing she was safe, I settled back down on the pillows. Although they hadn't seen me in a few years, we had all drank together enough times to no longer be embarrassed by my drunkenness. They each took it in stride and just went about their day.

On another occasion, I was so intoxicated while walking home that I thought I could change the dirt road to pavement to make it a more even surface to walk upon. I kept focusing on the road and seeing it change from dirt to pavement. That specific night, I had tried a few new drinks, and I can honestly say it was probably the closest I had ever come to alcohol poisoning.

As my father's alcoholism worsened during my twenties and he began using prescription drugs, I became more aware of the way alcohol profoundly affects every part of a body and a life. I also learned more about our family history. Alcoholism has been present in my family for many generations, and many in both lines of my family have gone from social drinkers to fully dependent upon alcohol just to get through each day.

As I got older, I found my tolerance for being around drugs and alcohol waning. It probably started the day I found my roommate in Las Vegas crawling on the floor, hand-picking dirt from the carpet after taking a "happy pill." It ended after seeing my father waste away year after year from drugs and alcohol.

In EMT school, all students were required to complete a few clinical rotations at an alcohol detoxification center to learn how to take vitals such as blood pressure, pulse, and respiratory rate. Many of the people in these centers have serious withdrawals, including delirium tremors (DTs), where they shake, sweat profusely, hallucinate, and have seizures. After my clinicals, I decided to continue volunteering at the center as a detox counselor and later was offered a part-time job. This gave me a better glimpse into the heavy toll of alcoholism on a person's mental and physical being.

It also caused me to finally stop drinking.

I felt like a hypocrite talking to people about alcohol rehab, only to later go out drinking with my friends. I began to cut back and cut back some more until I decided one day that it was just not worth it. Alcohol is a poison to the body; it dulls your senses and keeps you from being able to see life clearly. My work in emergency services also helped me to better understand my father and what he was going through much later in his life.

He called me once from a hospital room after moving to South Carolina and staying with my brother. "Lori, you need to come pick me up." He sounded frantic. He had injured his leg a few days before, and an infection had taken hold in his body, causing him to be admitted to the hospital.

"What is going on," I asked.

"They are trying to kill me!"

"What are you talking about?" I asked. "The hospital?"

"They nailed me to the floor! It is covered in bugs! You need to help me."

"Dad," I sighed, resting my head in my hand, "you were not nailed to the floor at the hospital."

"Don't argue with me!" he yelled. "They nailed me to the floor and wouldn't let me up. They're gonna kill me. Come get me!"

Shortly after being admitted to the hospital, he began hallucinating and having seizures from alcohol withdrawal. As soon as I heard his descriptions of what he believed was happening to him, I knew what was going on. I spoke to the nurse's office to give them more of my father's history in hopes that it would help them treat him. He was a difficult patient, even without hallucinations. I could not imagine how bad things were with the withdrawals.

My father died several years later, Memorial Day weekend in 2012. In the years between my middle school days and middle age, I would love to tell you that he changed—that he saw the harm he was causing to himself and others, and he got the help he really needed. But there is no happy ending here. My father died alone, addicted to both pills and alcohol, after a life of pain. When I was young, I avoided him because I was not able to separate his addiction from the man I once knew as a young child. He was manipulative, and I enabled his addiction because I remembered who he once was and could possibly be again.

Becoming an EMT changed all of that. As part of my training and my work at the detox center, I truly learned about addiction and its hold on so many people. And I learned how to best protect myself from those addictions. As a daughter, it was not my job to take the abuse just because it was my father dishing it out. And most importantly, sometimes the best way to help someone is to not help at all. I learned boundaries, and I used them to recreate a relationship with my father that lasted another fifteen years. Unfortunately, my father continued to spiral, and the relationship frayed to the point where it finally broke. I had not spoken to my father for three years when I was informed of his death.

I read in a book somewhere that addiction follows you from one life to another until you can break the cycle. Every time I thought of my father, I thought of that idea—we must break the cycles that keep us from moving forward. So, when my father died, I didn't break down and cry or regret not speaking to him for so long. I felt deep sorrow that he was never able to see his situation clearly, that he was unable to move past addiction. I was sad at the thought that he would have to face addiction again in his next life and only hoped that he would be able to break the cycle once and for all.

When I first learned about addiction, I lacked a true understanding of the hold it has on people. I felt constant frustration about why these people didn't just stop—stop taking the drugs, stop drinking. Why couldn't my father choose us over alcohol?

It made me so angry. If everything is so bad, why don't you stop?

I couldn't fathom why anyone would allow their life to unravel so spectacularly. And once a person did seek help and get clean, nine times out of ten, they would go back to drinking or using drugs again. I tried to find rational explanations, but they were never there.

I continued working at the detox center. I also started reading more about addiction. I tried to learn why this was so prevalent in our community and throughout the United States. I once read that meth changes the brain so completely that it takes up to two years to return to where you were before meth. Imagine that! When I read about someone going through withdrawal and then rehab and staying clean for six months or a year only to return to the drug that caused all their pain, I now understand better why it wasn't just a matter of willpower or making a decision because your family begged you to stop. It is something much deeper and more pervasive.

Addiction has wrecked more families than anything else I can recall. And many family members spend years trying to get help for the ones they love, followed by years of guilt that they failed. Many continue to help, time and again, hoping that it may be the last time their loved one goes through this pain. What I have learned about addiction is complex. For one, I have learned to be more empathetic to those who are going through addiction. I now believe that it must be one of the most difficult things to overcome. I no longer think, "Why don't you just quit?" That question came from a lack of understanding. Instead, I recognize the burden, the disease, for what it is and try not to be too harsh a judge.

Second, and equally important, is that I have learned that a person cannot and will not change until they are ready. There is no forcing someone to get help. They must see it as something they need to do first. And with this realization comes an even more difficult one—I don't have to enable someone with addiction. I have seen this time and again. I did it myself in my twenties. I enabled my father. I allowed him to manipulate me and get me to send him money or pay his rent or any number of other financial burdens. He cried, he yelled, he did whatever was needed for me to feel sadness or guilt so that I would do as he asked. After working at the detox center, I learned that I could love my father and wish him well without also allowing him to take advantage of me.

Much like the spirit in the firehouse, I set boundaries. I learned that sometimes the best way to help someone is to not help them at all. For those of us who have grown up to become helpers, this is an incredibly difficult lesson, but it is one that serves me well these many years later.

CHAPTER 9
Perception

It was a typical winter day. The roads were icy and snow-packed as my trainer, Siggy, and I transported a man to a Denver area hospital after he accidentally cut off his own hand. The man suffered from anxiety, and seeing the large bandage and lack of hand did not help his overall stress level.

I had a habit of pissing Siggy off. I called him "Mr. Crankypants," which probably didn't help, but it described him quite well. Siggy reminded me of my father—meaning that I routinely went back and forth between a desire to give him a hug and wanting to wring his neck. He was both a fun-loving, kind man and a curmudgeon all rolled into one. It just depended on the day.

I worked with Siggy as a brand-new rookie EMT through to paramedic school and later after I became a trainer myself. But in the beginning, I wasn't really the sharpest tack in the box, and Siggy was not afraid to tell me how much I sucked.

I drove the ambulance while Siggy attended to the patient in the back. Mostly Siggy worked to keep the man calm and provided pain medications as needed. We were in an old ambulance that tended to have regular maintenance issues. While driving in the snowstorm, I realized that the brakes were mushy—it took a bit of force to get the ambulance to stop.

I am not known for keeping the thoughts in my head from coming out of my mouth. So, me being me, I commented, "These brakes really suck."

Almost instantly, Siggy popped his head up from the back of the ambulance into the driver's compartment just inches from my head and said very softly, "It is probably best not to say anything that will *alarm* the patient further. He is nervous as it is and isn't getting better knowing that the brakes might fail."

Brilliant. Another point for the rookie.

AT SIGGY'S MEMORIAL service years later, I stood up to tell everyone a different story, one that most in the room would recognize well. We had taken a patient to St. Anthony's Hospital and dropped him off. It was the middle of the summer and was incredibly hot. I think our air conditioner was also broken, making this less than a fun day to begin with. The ambulance broke down a few miles away from the hospital on our way back home. Siggy, mechanically inclined, attempted to fix the problem but just got more and more frustrated as time went by. He ended up having a full-on meltdown in front of the ambulance as I sat in the passenger seat watching. Relatively new to the ambulance service at the time, I didn't yet know what this meltdown might mean for my safety, so I just stayed quiet and waited.

Finally, Siggy slammed the hood down, walked down the block, and turned a corner out of sight. This was before we had the ability to call someone with our Nextel direct connect phones to get advice, so I just sat there. He had to return, right? I waited and I waited, and finally, as I was about to give up and start walking myself, I saw Siggy turn the corner, heading back to the ambulance.

But this was a different Siggy.

First, he was whistling a jaunty little tune, and second, he had an ice cream cone in each hand. He got into the ambulance, just as happy as can be, handed me an ice cream cone, and proceeded to eat with a smile on his face. When he was done, he fixed the ambulance, and we were back on our way.

The reason this story was so important to me is that it truly illustrated Siggy's way. He was a very compassionate soul and could charm the very worst of patients. And although he earned the name of Mr. Crankypants, he also received more letters of thanks from patients than any other paramedic on the ambulance service. And he had the absolute best laugh—a full-body Santa Claus-style laugh.

During his memorial, so many people got up to talk about Siggy and how he had affected their lives. It hit me during the celebration of his life that while he was a cranky ole guy, it only took one or two interactions with him to leave a mark forever. And he routinely went out of his way to help people in the most unusual ways. He would come to your house and sit with you while you were ill or make you laugh when you were down. And the minute he knew that his crankypants nature was affecting your mood, he would change to jolly Siggy, whose mission was to make your day brighter.

If I had only allowed myself to see Siggy's cranky nature, I would have missed out on one of the kindest souls I have met in my lifetime. Had I gotten angry every time he yelled at me about something I did that he hated, my judgment would have been clouded, and I would have missed all the good times we had together.

Perception is a tricky thing. None of us truly know the people with whom we interact. Even in EMS, where you spend inordinate amounts of time together, sleeping in the same quarters during twenty-four- or forty-eight-hour shifts, we cannot know the inner workings of another's mind or truly understand how they came to be who they currently are.

Growing up, I did not know my grandfather well. I remember him as a quiet man who would sit in his rocking chair when we visited and would barely engage. He wasn't your typical grandfather type, full of excitement at being able to get to know his grandkids. Instead, he seemed rather disinterested. As a young child and a teenager, I often wondered why he didn't want to know us.

What had I done wrong?

Later, I learned that when he was a younger man, he had been an abusive alcoholic who hit not only his wife but his kids as well. I had a hard time reconciling the quiet man who sat alone with an abusive alcoholic. He had been in AA for most of his life after my grandmother threatened to leave him, so I had only known him sober. I didn't think very highly of my grandfather after learning about his drinking and abusive behavior. I judged him.

Even later, while doing research on our family history, I read a story written by my mother about my grandfather's childhood. His father, Henry, was clinically insane and extremely abusive to his family. He was a sadist who liked to create pain and suffering. In one instance, Henry made Leo, my grandfather, watch as he whipped a horse to death.

After years of abuse, Henry locked his three children up in the attic for three days without food or water while he beat and tortured his wife. If it hadn't been for a neighbor hearing the screams and reporting the incident, they may never have been found. Henry was taken away and institutionalized for a time following this incident but returned to the family at the end of his stay. At the age of fifteen, Leo ran away from home, established himself in Kansas, and sent for his mom and his younger sister.

Learning that my grandfather's childhood was so unstable and that he suffered so much abuse made me feel more sympathetic toward him. But I wondered how he could become abusive after all he had been through with his own father.

Upon further research on Leo's life, I came across some articles in the *Rocky Mountain News*. On the front page of every Colorado newspaper on February 16, 1946, there were pictures of a family of four that had died of carbon monoxide poisoning in their home the day before. My grandfather had purchased a new home for his growing family in Denver, Colorado. They had moved in on February 14, and the next morning, my grandfather kissed his two sons, his daughter, and his pregnant wife goodbye and left to go to work. Unknown to the family, a service worker had left a rag stuffed in a pipe after fumigating the home, and the house filled with carbon monoxide, killing the family. Leo returned home that evening to find his entire family had perished in the home.

He was the only survivor.

Learning about my grandfather's life and the tragedies he endured felt like peeling back an onion to find the layers beneath. Before he became the quiet old man I knew who barely spoke to us, his life was a mixture of triumphs and tragedies that shaped and molded him. I now understand why he was later a distant father to my mother and why he never really tried to get to know us. How could he get close to anyone again after such a horrible loss? I also understand how he could become an alcoholic, even after what his father had done to him. Nothing blurs reality and the past like drugs and alcohol.

Our perception of others is based upon our experiences. Unless we are willing to spend the time peeling back the onion, we cannot fully know someone. I often wonder how different my father might have been if both his parents hadn't died when he was sixteen years old. Would he have been a happier person? I also wonder about all the layers I never got to explore.

This is where being a watcher comes in handy. I will have a different perspective depending upon where I am viewing what is going on. As a medic, my perception may be different from the door than it would be inside the room. Standing closer to the patient will provide me with one story, while remaining farther away from the patient tells me something else. Looking at the scene from multiple perspectives gives me a broader picture. This is why firefighters try to see at least three sides of a building when responding to a structure fire—they don't want to focus on one problem only to learn that a much bigger problem exists on the other side of the building.

I could have continued to judge my grandfather for his past actions without ever understanding what he went through in his young life. I could have judged Siggy from the first time he yelled at me for no reason in the ambulance, but if I had done that, I never would have gotten to know the good man behind the mask.

Although I understand this intellectually, perception is a difficult thing. I believe in first impressions, but aren't those quick judgments as well? I know that I have judged people harshly in the past. I also know that I don't trust easily. But above all, I know that judgment and lack of trust can also be detrimental to my overall growth. What can I say? I am a work in progress.

I doubt if Siggy really knew or understood how many people he affected. It is hard to know what our actions will do to others or how they will react or be affected. One thing I do know is that my actions will create perceptions that will be both true and false, and my judgments of others will blind me to the beauty within. I would love to have the ability to positively influence even half the lives that Siggy touched while he was with us on this earth. It's even more amazing to realize that he accomplished all of that while being Mr. Crankypants.

CHAPTER 10
COURAGE

I HAVE ALWAYS loved fire. I love the way it moves. I love the way it breathes. I love the way it consumes. Not in the way an arsonist might, but in a way that can see beauty in darkness. Not only do I watch and analyze people and their actions, I watch and analyze how disasters form and what moves them to do what they do so that I can learn and respond. Fire has always been my favorite.

My first structure fire occurred when I was a brand-new EMT and volunteer firefighter for the Franktown Fire Department. I was all decked out in my shiny new yellow bunker gear for the first time.

I was too new to go into the building while it was on fire, so I assisted outside with changing out the self-contained breathing apparatus (SCBA) harnesses, and I provided refreshments to other firefighters. It was so cold outside that the minute firefighters left the building, their gloves froze in place, and the harness froze to the air bottle, requiring us to remove the entire apparatus instead of just changing out the bottles.

At the end of the fire, as the building still smoldered, the fire chief finally had a chance to look around. He took one look at me, shook his head, and laughed.

"Hodges, you're embarrassing me," he said with a look at my brand-new bright yellow bunker gear. "Go inside and roll around in the ashes for a while." I grinned at him and started toward the door of the burned structure. He didn't have to tell me twice.

The first time I went to Loveland Field Days and experienced the burn room was life-altering. I remember the fear before going in—the fear of the unknown. This was a controlled environment, but it would still involve an active fire. We partnered up and checked each other's gear before filing into the room and kneeling down. Once given the thumbs up, one of the instructors ignited the fire.

It started slowly, curling around the eaves of the adjacent room, moving smoothly along the ceiling until flame covered everything above us. I was struck by how the fire seemed to breathe in and out, sometimes growing and other times retreating. The smoke became thick above us, slowly moving down toward our heads, and the room's temperature increased significantly as we breathed through our SCBAs.

We stayed in that environment until the smoke and heat became too intense, and then the instructors ushered us outside as they extinguished the fire. Once outside, I realized that I had not felt fear while in the fire—it was only before. It was the thought of what could go wrong or what might happen that made me anxious. But once inside, the fire mesmerized me. I just sat and watched as it crept through the room, curling and flowing beautifully.

Later, while doing training rotations in another fire room, I met up with several firefighters on the outside after the exercise.

"Look at this," one young firefighter said, face beaming. He had his ruined helmet in his hands. "I stayed inside so long that my helmet melted. None of you could do that."

"Why would I want to do that?" I said.

"You are just upset that you couldn't do it," he boasted.

Unfortunately for him, the instructor did not see things his way. "It isn't courageous to stay in a building until your equipment melts," the instructor said to everyone. "It's stupid. You put every one of your team at risk by taking chances like that." The instructor walked up to the young firefighter to get his attention. "Never do that again."

When I was a little girl, I had a recurring nightmare of a man staring at me just a few inches from my face, whispering to me. He was an older man, in his sixties, with cigarette breath. He would speak softly, right in front of my face. I would wake night after night in complete terror and then try to stay awake for as long as possible so that I wouldn't see the man again.

The nightmare went on for years. It never really made sense to me why the vision was so terrifying. It was just a face close to mine, whispering. The words would echo in my brain, but I don't remember it being the words that were so frightening—it was the man and the closeness. And to this day, that vision still gives me the creeps.

Ever since I can remember, I feel uncomfortable when people are too close to me. I will often take a step back when someone leans in to tell me something. Picture a physical plastic bubble surrounding my body. When people get too close, they push on the bubble, causing me to lose balance and step back. In a few cases, I have had to put my hand up and tell someone that they are in my space and need to back up.

Don't even get me started on the huggers out there. Inevitably, they will find a way. They come up, raising their arms quickly and spreading them for the big embrace while saying, "I know you're not a hugger, but I am going to hug you anyway." Meanwhile, I either cringe through the experience or find a way out of it. Patrick Swayze was right in *Dirty Dancing*—we each have our own dance space, and I am someone who does *not* like it when others enter my dance space.

Seriously, back the fuck up!

Nowadays, people see me and start to spread their arms wide for a hug, but something in my presence stops them. Inevitably, I get ready for the hug only to have them stop suddenly, arms halfway up before lowering them again. I guess I have gotten better at changing my energy to better communicate when a hug is either welcome or unwelcome.

I had my first boyfriend in first grade. He was one of my good friends, and at that age, that was all that mattered. Tommy was my boyfriend through the fourth grade. He used to call me up and break up with me, only to call back later and ask to be my boyfriend again. I always said yes until the day he didn't call back. He knew I would always be there, but I came to realize that he did not feel the same.

In sixth grade, my boyfriend broke up with me after a year because he thought I was fat. We went from being close friends and doing everything together to one day being nothing to one another. When he told me he was breaking up with me, I didn't get angry and didn't fight for myself. I was anything but fat in sixth grade, but regardless, I should have stood up for myself. Instead, I internalized the rejection and blamed myself for not being good enough.

It wasn't until my twenties that I purposefully tried to open myself up again to establish a deep connection with someone. I didn't trust relationships, but I desperately wanted to trust again.

At the age of twenty-one, I was still a social drinker. I enjoyed going out with friends drinking and partying. I was exactly the opposite of who I am now—I was extremely extroverted and incredibly social. I'd get up on a table and dance if I liked the song on the jukebox. Alcohol amplified my nature, allowing me to act without fear.

One night, after drinking with a bunch of friends, we all walked back home from the bar to our respective apartments. This was the same night where I tried to change the dirt road to pavement with my mind, so it is easy to say I was incredibly intoxicated. Once we got to my street, I said goodbye to my friends and waved as I turned down my street and walked alone the rest of the way to my apartment. I unlocked the door, went inside, and promptly passed out in bed.

Later in the night, I groggily woke feeling disoriented. At first, I thought I might be dreaming, but as my hazy brain cleared, I realized that one of my male friends who I had gone out drinking with that night was in my bed, lying on top of me. He had entered my apartment, entered my room, removed my clothes, and sexually assaulted me while I was passed out in bed.

I have snapshots of what happened that night as I drifted in and out of consciousness. In my state, I was wholly unable to defend myself, and the so-called friend took advantage of my condition to do whatever he wanted with my body.

When I woke the next morning, he was gone. I tried to convince myself that nothing had really happened to me, but my body told me a different story.

I wouldn't admit to myself that I'd been assaulted. I was young, I had been drinking, and he was supposed to be a friend. Instead, I blamed myself for being so vulnerable to such an act, even though he had entered my apartment without my knowledge or permission, and he took something that wasn't offered.

In the morning, I acted as if nothing had happened and went about my life. I just wanted to forget that it ever happened and move on. I wasn't broken. I wasn't injured. It was just something that had happened to me. What I didn't know then is that assault comes in many forms, and although I didn't have physical injuries, I was, in fact, injured. I also didn't know that the man who had assaulted me had taken the time after the assault to paint a horrific picture of me to everyone we knew. He told tall tales to all our mutual friends, which caused each of them to slowly distance themselves from me. It wasn't until much later that I learned all the lies that had been told about me.

Later, I dated a man for three months and then felt comfortable enough to have him come stay with me in my apartment for the weekend. At the end of the weekend, he told me he was getting back together with his ex-girlfriend.

At the *end* of the weekend!

I should have picked up my baseball bat and expressed my displeasure at being thrown away. At the very least, I should have kicked him out of my home. Instead, I was understanding and sad.

I did not stand up for myself. I froze. I did nothing and waited for the pain to pass.

And on and on it goes. All the way back to my first boyfriend, who'd call and break up with me on a whim and then call later to ask if we could get back together—me always saying yes.

I have only had a handful of relationships in my life, and when I have met someone who is kind and compassionate, I have always found a reason to run. I am terrified to trust anyone again, to get too close. For years, I have stayed away from any type of close relationship.

One of my favorite book characters is a woman named Flora Dane in the Detective D. D. Warren books by Lisa Gardner. Flora starts out as one of the victims that Detective Warren helps. She is abducted in the story by a psychopath and spends a year locked in a coffin-sized box. Once she escapes her abuser, she develops a protective mechanism. She learns not only how to fight back but also how to lure predators in and how to kill them. There is something about this character that I really love.

Stick with me here.

I am not saying I want to become a vigilante killer. Instead, I respect that she is able to take something awful that happened to her and build power from it. She makes sure she will never again be anyone's victim. I have so much respect for that.

For me, I let a man assault me without ever confronting him or holding him accountable. I let him crush my reputation, and I let him cause me to lose friends—I just walked away. By allowing people to treat me with such disrespect and then just throw me away, I allowed them to turn me into a true victim.

I didn't fight back.

I allowed the men who mistreated me to walk away and to do it again to someone else.

This is a regret I have to this day.

I did not understand self-worth or trauma at the time and often chalked my experiences up to the cost of living. I also didn't understand the value of friendship and the trust that comes with such a relationship. I used to think that I deserved what happened to me if I got drunk. But it took the memory of another interaction to illustrate true friendship.

When a few of my high school friends stayed with me in my apartment while visiting from Colorado, I went to bed after drinking with them for a few hours. After a bit, the bed started spinning, and I felt I might be sick. So, I tried to move to the edge of the bed to hang my head off the side but had trouble getting up. Within a few moments, my friend Jon came running into my room, yelling at me to turn over. He must have heard me in distress, and he acted immediately. He sat with me that night and made sure I didn't get sick or choke or anything worse. He was vigilant, making sure that I made it through the night.

I remember this every time I begin to blame myself for what happened to me when I was younger, when a so-called friend assaulted me. I remember the selfless actions of my friend Jon. A friend takes care of you and ensures that no harm comes to you. The person who assaulted me was never my friend, and he should not have gotten away with what he did to me.

I never want to be a victim again. I want to be more like Flora Dane—a fighter and a survivor. I don't want things to happen *to* me; I want to shape my own destiny. I want to stand up when it is important to stand up, and I want to speak out when I feel wronged or when others have been wronged.

In my work, I do this well. I have a reputation for being unafraid to speak my mind to those in positions of authority. My boss even told me that some consider me to be a bit of a bulldog. In my work, I am not meek or mild, and I do not stand down—even when I probably should. But at home, in my personal life, I still struggle with letting people in, and I struggle with standing up when people let me down. I tend to walk away—if I feel threatened, I happily let my amygdala take over, allowing me to quickly exit the scene and never look back.

I struggle with fear.

The side effect of this is that I have very few close relationships. I would like to let people in more, but first, I must learn to fight for myself as much as I fight in my work. I need to be open and welcoming while also being a bulldog when it counts the most. I need to conquer my fears and let my prefrontal cortex take the reins now and again.

CHAPTER 11

Trust

On **April Fool's** Day 2016, at approximately 9 p.m., my phone rang.

"Hello, this is Lori."

"Hey, it's Braden."

"What's up?" I was working as the emergency manager for Larimer County, and Braden was one of our partners in EMS.

"I need your help. I am on scene of a medical call. The patient is exhibiting symptoms consistent with Ebola and has a travel history that leads us to believe she could have been exposed."

"Bullshit," I laughed.

This was at the height of the Ebola outbreak and the scare moving through the United States was very real. If true, this would be huge! But it was also April Fool's Day, and Braden was known to joke around—a lot!

"Seriously, Lori, this isn't a joke. I am literally standing in front of the house right now. The patient is inside, and we are working out the logistics of transporting her to the hospital and where to take her."

I shook my head again. "Bullshit."

Absolutely nothing was going to make me believe that out of all days we would have an Ebola-suspect patient, it would be April Fool's Day, and that Braden, of all people, would be the one to be on scene. No freaking way.

Braden laughed at me, swore up and down he was not joking, and tried to get me to believe in what he was saying. After a few more minutes, knowing he wasn't getting anywhere, he hung up.

Within a minute, the phone rang again from an unknown number.

"Hello, this is Lori," I said, with a smile in my voice.

"Lori, this is Jim, the incident commander on scene of the medical call Braden called you about. I absolutely assure you that this is a real call."

"Well, shit."

Although I was relatively certain at that point that this was now a real call, I admittedly still had the thought in the back of my head that Braden had just had one of his paramedic friends call me to up the ante on the best April Fool's joke ever. But no, it was a real call. On April Fool's Day. With Braden, the resident EMS jokester,

I took down all the information and got to work assisting the responders and preparing for the media storm that would hit our county if the patient tested positive for Ebola. Luckily, we received the negative test results overnight and the patient was treated and released from the hospital before anyone woke the next day.

While riding my bike home in Las Vegas in my early twenties, I saw a woman in a wheelchair at a stoplight. Her wheelchair seemed stuck at the curb, so I went over and helped her get the chair unstuck and assisted her across the street.

"Thank you," she said. "I am a visiting professor at the university, and I've lost my identification and all my money."

"Can I help you get to the university?" I asked.

"They are closed for Thanksgiving. I couldn't get here on time. I just need some money to get through the weekend."

Being a poor college student, I didn't have any money. But I also couldn't just leave her there. This was 1990, before cell phones and the internet, or even really computers for that matter, so options were really limited on how best to help. It was entirely plausible that her story was true and that she was stuck in an unknown city with no options.

I was a naive twenty-year-old who still tried to believe in the goodness of every person. It was also Thanksgiving, so what better way to show my thanks for all I had than to help someone in need? I liked the idea of doing a good deed for a perfect stranger.

"I only live a few blocks away," I said. "You could stay with me if you need a place to stay."

At first, she looked at me strangely and said that she couldn't possibly stay with me, that she just needed some money. But I was insistent and wore her down. I walked next to her wheelchair with my bike as we traveled from UNLV to my one-bedroom apartment a few blocks away.

The entire way there, she kept saying, "You should never do this again." Over and over, she kept telling me what a bad idea it was to have a stranger stay with me. The walk was long enough for me to realize that she was right. What the hell was I thinking? And if the person I was trying to help was nervous for me, it had to be a bad idea. But I couldn't back out now!

Once we got to the apartment, I fixed some dinner and set up my room for her to sleep. I decided to sleep on the couch by the door because I had realized how precarious the situation really was by that point, and I wanted to have both a quick exit as well as be in a position to see if she robbed me blind in the middle of the night.

I am happy to say that she did not steal from me. I didn't sleep much, but the night was uneventful, and, in the morning, I took her back to UNLV, where she said she would find someone to help her. I felt good being able to help but was greatly relieved once I was able to walk away and go back home. Crisis averted! And she didn't kill me in my sleep or rob me, so I felt that my Pollyanna worldview was intact.

Almost a year later, while walking along the Las Vegas Strip with some friends, I looked over and saw the same exact woman panhandling. I stopped and watched her for a few minutes as she got out of her wheelchair and walked over to pick something off the street before returning to the wheelchair to continue asking people for assistance.

All at once, I saw the situation from a year earlier more clearly. She had told me that story about being stranded in hopes that I would give her money. It was a con. And being young and poor, I never even thought of giving her money. I just thought of giving her shelter. I realized why she seemed so insistent that I never do something like that again. She knew that it could be dangerous with the wrong person.

I froze when I saw her. A deep anger built up inside me. In that moment, my sense of the world as one with good, honest people who will do the right thing when tested was crushed to dust. I felt a huge sense of betrayal. The last of my naivete disappeared. Pollyanna had left the building.

I did not speak with the woman, but I did make sure we made eye contact before I walked away. Who knows if she recognized me, but I felt better thinking she knew that I knew about the lie. This was the last time in a long time I gave someone my trust. From that point forward, I was constantly on guard for lies and manipulations, thinking that everyone was out to either trick me as part of a joke, or scam me out of money.

With age, I better understand her position, and the anger has faded. Instead, I now see a woman without a home doing what she needed to survive one more day, and maybe on that Thanksgiving, I gave her one night of safety that she may not have had on any other day. I guess that is okay.

Did I allow this incident with the stranger in Vegas to keep me from helping people again? No. If I allowed that one incident to prevent me from helping other people experiencing homelessness because I don't want to be duped again, then the person who truly needs help will not get it. Instead, I now give what I can to those in need without any expectation that I know what is truly going on. Perhaps it's someone who is trying to manipulate the situation for personal gain. Perhaps it is someone who lost their job and has four children at home. If I give to both, I at least know at the end of it all there is one person I was able to help to get to better circumstances.

Age gives you the knowledge to see these differences clearly and make decisions while maintaining faith in humanity. While paramedicine showed me the dark side of human nature at times, it also showed me the light. Disasters start with a horrible act but always—always—end with the absolute best of humanity. Communities come together to help their fellow neighbors, those unaffected donate their money or volunteer their time to help strangers, and multiple agencies work together to ensure a swift and complete recovery. In the difficult work of emergency response and emergency management, the lesson here is to see beyond the challenge or the call in front of you. Look for the beauty that comes after that call. Look for the good in the bad. It is always there.

PHASE 3:
BECOMING

How fleeting is anyone's experience relative to the broad life span of the planet! And yet we each partake of that whole. Indeed, there are those who give themselves so deeply to this world, who open their souls so fully to each chance encounter, who so thoroughly resolve not to shrink from any of the uncanny textures or flavors or feels that this life offers, that from these many encounters their hearts distill a mysterious elixir, an invisible tonic that streams out from their eyes to refresh all that they look upon, waking a secret and long slumbering sentience in things, quickening a pulse deep within the ground wherever they wander.

—David Abram, foreword to *Wild Love for the World*

CHAPTER 12

Standing Up

In the mid-1990s, as a relatively new EMT, I responded with my paramedic partner to a condo unit in the Keystone Ski Resort for the report of a suicide attempt. Upon arrival we found a young man and woman, both upset but without visible injuries. After an examination we found that the woman had a few scratches on her wrist, superficial at best, with no active bleeding and no other health concerns. She said that she had gotten upset at her boyfriend and had threatened to cut her wrists with a butter knife but hadn't really meant it. She was just angry and upset.

"We need to take you to the hospital and get you checked out," I said, knowing something else might be going on and hoping to get her away from her boyfriend to talk.

"No, I am really fine. We were both upset, and I was being stupid." Her boyfriend agreed and said he would look out for her.

Clearly, she had been crying and was not in a great emotional state. I felt uneasy about the scene, but my senior partner told me we couldn't force her to come with us and that we didn't have enough of a reason to take her in. After trying for several more minutes and getting the same response, we left the scene to return to quarters. As soon as we left, I felt those uneasy butterflies in my stomach and chest, my intuition telling me that something just wasn't right. I felt that if we left, something bad would happen.

As soon as we got to quarters and pulled into the station, we received a second call to the same address. The woman had slit her wrists. This time with a knife that could cause the damage she'd intended. This was one of a few examples of a time when I deferred to a more seasoned medic and ignored my gut only to learn that my gut instinct was always right. We bandaged the patient's wrists and transported her to the hospital for both medical and psychiatric evaluation.

When I was young, my father thought it was funny to tease my little brother or talk down to my mother. My father would recruit my older brother in his games that were designed to belittle my younger brother, Billy. They would continue picking at him until he either lashed out in anger or broke down into tears. Either emotion elicited more laughter from the two of them. I don't remember participating in the teasing or bullying, but I do remember laughing at their actions and doing nothing to stop the torment.

Back then, I worshipped my father. He was the fun dad who tried to make us laugh. He had not yet become the scary dad he would in middle school. So, I went along with all of it, trying my hardest to please him. I even remember my father making jokes about my mom's weight and all of us kids laughing, thinking at the time that it was all so much fun.

In middle school, there was a student named Mandy that all the other kids teased. For one Halloween, she dressed as a Smurf, and following that day, whenever people saw her, they sang the Smurf song as she walked down the halls. The teasing was relentless. She would hurry through the halls to get from class to her locker and to her next class as fast as possible, tightly clutching her books and keeping her head down. On more than one occasion, the teasing became too much, and she lashed out at her tormentors, only for more laughter to follow.

But what I remember most is all the bystanders. The people who did not participate in the teasing but did nothing about it. I am ashamed to say that I was one of those people. I witnessed relentless torment and felt bad for Mandy, but I never intervened. In the 1980s, bullying was a part of school, and it wasn't monitored the way that it is today. It never occurred to me back then to get involved. In some way I must have reasoned that if I didn't participate I couldn't be blamed.

To this day, my inaction bothers me. I was just as much to blame for her torment as those who had actively participated. I should have stood up for Mandy and stopped the abuse even if it meant abuse for me. It was the right thing to do.

A few years later, at a high school party at my house, I walked into my bedroom to find a girl passed out on my bed with several drunk students in the room preparing to cut off her hair. She was known for her beautiful, long blond hair, and this group of kids thought it would be funny to cut it all off while she was passed out drunk. I saw the silver on the scissors wrapping around her hair.

I recalled Mandy.

I did not hesitate.

"What the hell do you think you're doing?" I yelled from the doorway.

They all jumped at the interruption. I took the opportunity to storm into the room and rip the scissors out of the hand of the kid holding them.

"What is wrong with you?" I screamed. "Get the hell out of my house!"

As they quickly left, I made sure each one knew what a piece of shit I thought they were.

Not one of them probably remembers that night since they were all intoxicated—not the girl with the long blond hair or the group that thought it would be funny to take that beauty away. It was the first time that I really stood up for someone that could not stand up for themselves. And it felt right.

At my ten-year high school reunion, I spoke to a fellow former student who told me she had deeply feared me in high school. When I walked down the halls, she'd turn around and walk the other way. She thought I would beat her up if confronted.

I was horrified. I have never been in a fight in my life, nor did I think it was possible for me to instill fear in others. One of my fears, however, is that the high school I remember is not the high school others remember. What if I was someone's bully? What if I caused torment to others and just never realized it? All those years she had avoided me in the halls because she thought I would hurt her. She didn't give me any one example of a time that I was mean or where I threatened her, and she didn't say I was a bully. She just said that she feared me and had avoided me when she saw me.

I tried to think back to determine whether there was a time when I was intentionally mean, unintentionally mean, participated in bullying behavior, anything. Honestly, I was rather self-absorbed in high school, so all I could remember were my own stupid problems. I honestly don't think I was a bully in high school. I was not part of the cool crowd, but I wasn't reviled either. I was neither the bully nor the one being bullied. I was a middle-of-the-road student who hung out with kids from all the different cliques. I was known as the girl who threw a great party and as "that drummer chick." Nothing extraordinary and nothing to draw too much attention. I remember having a really great time in high school.

At the end of the conversation, I realized that her fear was more related to how I presented myself in high school. I walked with purpose (on purpose). I had been taught early in life by my mom to walk with confidence and make eye contact. I was just as insecure as all the other students, but I apparently did a great job of hiding it.

Since that conversation, however, I have been much more aware of my treatment of others. I have a resting bitch face, though, so sometimes I inadvertently make people think I am pissed at them just because I am not paying attention to my face. But I have also been more intentional in calling out bullying behavior when I see it, and I try to include those who may feel excluded. I don't know if the way I walk or talk still affects those around me, and I don't know if anyone considers my actions to be bullying—I hope not—but I am more aware that this is a possibility that my actions could cause a perception that is not reality.

When I was a trainee as part of an incident management team, I met a man named Marc, who was a Type I incident commander for a federal wildfire team. I worked with his team on several occasions as both a trainee and an emergency manager. I grew to respect Marc greatly, not just because of his knowledge as an incident commander, but because of how he treated his team and trainees like me. He would stop by at least once a day just to check in and make sure I was taking care of myself. He stressed self-care all the time and watched out for everyone around him.

Many years later, that same kind man drove to a secluded spot on a road away from home and killed himself. He died in January 2008 of a self-inflicted gunshot wound.

Most people who knew him were shocked. It had never occurred to any of us that he suffered from depression or that he would ever get to the point where he felt suicide was the only answer. He was another reminder that you never truly know what is going on in someone else's life. Each of us shares a tiny bit with others, and if they stick around long enough, you learn a bit more. But there is always a side that is hidden from others. Maybe one friend knows a side of you, and another friend knows a completely different side. Both are true, and they are just two parts of a greater whole. I am sure that Marc's close friends had seen something along the way, maybe they had worried a time or two about Marc and how he was doing. I wonder if his attentiveness to others was a reflection of his feelings of isolation or even PTSD after all he had done and seen.

What I want to tell all these people now is that I SEE YOU.

From one invisible person to another, I see you. You are not alone.

I think of Mandy whenever I see abuse of any kind, and I hope to be the person who will always stand up and intervene instead of being a silent bystander. I think of Marc whenever I enter the Emergency Operations Center and witness the stress of the individuals in the room. I strive to take the time to do what he taught me—to go around the room and check to make sure everyone is doing well, that they are taking care of themselves and one another. I also make sure my staff knows to do the same with me. Everyone needs someone looking out for them, making sure that they not only get through the day but that they know the next day will be brighter because there are others who have their backs.

CHAPTER 13

Inquiry

"**W**HAT HAPPENED?"

"You were in a skiing accident."

"Where are we?"

"We are in an ambulance heading toward Denver."

"Why aren't we moving?"

"The ambulance broke down. Someone is on the way to help us."

The patient seemed satisfied. He stopped looking around and rested his head back on the gurney mattress and closed his eyes. A few seconds later, he opened his eyes, looked confused, and tried to sit up.

"What happened?"

"You were in a skiing accident."

"Where are we?"

"We are in an ambulance heading toward Denver."

"Why aren't we moving?"

"The ambulance broke down. Don't worry. We have help on the way."

"Oh, okay." He lay back down and seemed content once again. A few seconds passed before the cycle repeated again. "What happened?"

Sighing, I closed my eyes and breathed deeply in and out through my nose before answering. I glanced out the window in hopes of seeing another ambulance coming up the interstate so we could get back on the road. It wasn't the patient's fault, so losing patience wouldn't do any good. But of course, if I did lose my patience, all would be forgiven. Or, more accurately, forgotten in about ten seconds when the patient's short-term memory erased once again. He had been in a skiing accident and suffered from a closed-head injury causing short-term memory difficulties. So, if I were really bored and wanted to have a little fun, I could mix it up a little.

"What happened?"

"You were attacked by a gang of bikers."

"Where?"

"Sturgis, South Dakota."

"Why would I go to a biker rally?"

"People do crazy things when they turn sixty."

"I'm sixty?"

"Yeah. But you don't look it."

"What happened?"

"You were in a mosh pit that went bad."

"What's a mosh pit?"

"It doesn't matter, really."

Let's face it; these beat the hell out of the real reason why he was in an ambulance heading to a Level I Trauma Center, which is that he was trying to get on the show *Jackass* and ended up falling from the ski gondola, breaking his back and injuring his head.

Jackass indeed!

To be clear, I would never intentionally mess with my patient—at least not one with a closed-head injury. I am paranoid enough to believe that their short-term memory would begin to improve, and the one thing they would remember is the last thing I said. Then, when rolling them into the emergency room, the doctor would ask me what happened, and the patient would yell, "I was skydiving and my parachute didn't open. Can you believe that?"

Inevitably, I would get the doctor stare and head shake—the one that tells you that you are a waste of space on this earth, and you should be removed from society. So, for the fiftieth time, I answered the same questions, fully knowing it would come again in three . . . two . . . one . . .

"What happened?"

The questions continued after transferring the patient to a working ambulance, but they changed. Now the patient asked a series of ten questions in the same order each time, and the questions came in a loop. Once he finished the last question, there was a short pause before he began again from the top.

Therefore, once we were well underway, I took out a notepad and wrote the patient a note with the list of questions he had been asking. They came in the same order every time, so the note had the questions in order with my answers. The next time the patient asked, "What happened?" I told him to read the note in his hand. He looked at the note, then looked at me and said, "How did you know I was going to ask these questions?"

I had effectively stopped the loop of ten questions and narrowed it down to two.

My partner pulled into St. Anthony's Central Hospital, and we wheeled the patient's gurney into a trauma room with about ten people waiting. It was a teaching hospital, so many of the people were students.

I provided the room with my report, and we transferred the patient from the pram to a waiting bed. The doctor approached the patient and asked, "Can you tell me what happened?"

The patient shook his head, raised his right arm, and said, "No, but this note will tell you everything you need to know."

The entire room burst into laughter.

HEAD INJURIES ARE common in Summit County. The county is known for its outdoor activities—skiing, snowboarding, biking, kayaking, and hiking. These are also some of the most interesting injuries as a paramedic. They can cause a patient to perseverate (ask the same questions again and again) or cause them to completely change their personality.

My partner and I once responded to an eighty-year-old woman who had fallen and hit her head while getting into her car in the parking lot. When we arrived she seemed fine, but we took her to the clinic just to make sure. Halfway to our location, the sweet eighty-year-old lady turned into a WWE wrestler and decided to beat the shit out of my partner treating her in the back of the ambulance.

The brain is a beautiful and marvelous thing.

My brain works in a nonlinear fashion. Imagine a computer browser with multiple windows open all at once with a virus actively attacking the computer—that is my brain. This is why I ask so many questions and seek more information. It helps me to process a situation and determine the best outcome. Paramedicine was a good place for me for these reasons. While it exists as part of a paramilitary organization, most paramedics are systems thinkers; they routinely need to make quick decisions with little information in new circumstances without any assistance or guidance.

I don't typically believe things I first hear without further study. This, coupled with my trust issues, makes me question the world in ways that many others just accept. Some think I am arguing with them or challenging them. But in my mind, I am just trying to put all the pieces together I wish to understand, which will lead to acceptance of new information.

I am a big reader. I read anything and everything. I even bought a book about banned books and read all of them as well. My favorite book of all time is *Fahrenheit 451*—a book about banned books that has also been a banned book. Most excellent.

At one point in the story, a woman decides to burn in her home along with her books instead of leaving to safety. The lead character, Firefighter Guy Montag, muses to himself, "There must be something in books, things we can't imagine, to make a woman stay in a burning house." Montag truly understands for the first time the power of knowledge and the ability to think critically.

Anyone who doesn't routinely ask questions and seek information and understanding is someone who I believe will be easily led astray. These are the people who believe in conspiracy theories, who are easily manipulated, and who disappear because they willingly followed someone else straight into a cult. This was me when I allowed the homeless woman to stay at my home without fully understanding the dangers and realizing it was all a con.

In a briefing about extremist terrorism, I was told that people are taught to not question the teaching of a specific religion, and if they do, they are at risk of being killed for daring to question. Imagine that. If the teachings cannot be questioned, my first thought is, "What are they trying to hide?"

See what I did there?

My first instinct was to ask a question.

If the teachings are true, then they should be able to stand up to scrutiny. Right? It is a good thing I was born in Colorado and to parents who were open to questions. There is no doubt I would have been killed in a matter of minutes if I had lived in an environment where questions were not allowed.

I worked as a liaison officer on an incident management team on a wildfire several years ago. The fire was in the forest, but it was threatening homes. At one point, a member of the team came in and said that another fire had been reported on the Park County line and structures were burning. Suddenly, the operations section started to shift resource priorities to the other fire—from the information they received, the new fire seemed to be a bigger concern. While this was going on, however, I decided to call the Park County Dispatch Center. In the short call, I learned that an outbuilding was on fire, but it hadn't spread to the forest, and resources were on scene. In essence, the new fire was a nonissue. We were about to shift a bunch of resources from a fire that had the potential to affect homes and people for what was essentially a shed on fire. When I asked the team member where he got the information about the fire, he said he had seen it on a blog post.

Grrrr.

In the end, it was a good lesson for the entire team about ensuring that our information is coming from reliable sources before changing tactics or resource decisions. We must move fast and make decisions quickly, but that doesn't mean we shouldn't do everything in our power to ensure we have enough information to make the best decisions possible. We do this by asking questions.

One of my most common statements is, "I don't know about that." I just realized last year how much I say this. In most cases, when someone is trying to convince me of something, I will scrunch up my face and say, "I don't know about that." But then I also look it up to try to determine whether what I am being told is correct.

The reason all of this is important is that I believe that we must all use critical thinking skills when we are living our lives and never be afraid to ask questions. If someone is afraid of your questions, it is their ignorance, not yours. And don't be afraid of being judged harshly. Do not let that stop you. Question authority. Seek truth. Ask the hard questions.

And if you cannot do that, I sincerely hope that isn't Kool-Aid in your red Solo cup.

CHAPTER 14

Belief

Early in my career, I manned an ambulance that was stationed at Keystone Resort. On one of our trips to pick up a patient from the ski slopes, we picked up a young man who had broken his back after hitting a tree at high speed. We brought him into the clinic and then later picked him back up to transport him to a hospital in Denver, about one and a half hours away.

Throughout it all, the patient refused any and all pain medications. I could tell that the pain was excruciating. His face had sweat at the temples, and he would wince and grit his teeth every time we went over a bump in the road. In between the bumps, however, he would lie on the bed and smile up at the ceiling.

"Are you sure you don't want me to give you just a little pain medicine?" I asked. "It could help take the edge off, or I could give you something to help you relax."

He smiled again and looked me in the eye. "No, I'm good, thank you."

I thought maybe he was a recovering addict, refusing pain medications due to their addictive traits. "Is there anything else I could do to try to make you more comfortable?" I asked, trying again. "I can see you smiling, but I know you are in pain."

"I am a student at Naropa," he said, describing the university in Boulder, Colorado, that has programs that combine Eastern and Western thought with experiential learning. "I am studying Buddhism right now, and my homework for this weekend is to smile."

Smile.

He just needed to practice smiling. So, instead of taking pain medication, he had been doing his best to smile through the pain and discomfort from his injury until we reached the hospital.

"I am pretty certain your instructor would give you a pass," I said with a short laugh. "I doubt that breaking your back falls into the lesson plan."

"I think I'll be good," he said again before looking back at the ceiling and smiling.

For the rest of the transport, I felt a mixture of admiration and compassion for the young man. I would have taken the medication and excused it away because of the seriousness of the injury, but this young man felt a deep conviction in his studies and his beliefs. He braved the pain of a broken back and worked to see the beauty in the event while also turning pain into peace. All while keeping a smile on his face. It was remarkable.

In late 2018, at the age of forty-seven, I went into the emergency room for the fourth time with chest pain. I had been having chest pain off and on for a few years. At first, my doctors told me that a previous pulmonary embolism could cause a feeling of anxiety in the chest, so that was probably the cause. Even the thought of another embolism caused me anxiety. As I said previously, one in three people who experience a pulmonary embolism do not live to later write a book about the experience (I had already had two). I also knew that fear of the next medical emergency was constantly bouncing around in my brain.

I accepted the initial diagnosis of anxiety the first few times I went to the ER. But the chest pain continued to come and go. I went to my primary-care physician about the pain. He suggested going on anxiety medication because there wasn't anything that the doctors could find that was physically wrong with me. I denied his diagnosis and went home again with no answers.

By 2018, after several doctor visits and multiple emergency room visits, I was quite frankly sick of it. I knew from my years as a paramedic that you should always take chest pain seriously. I knew that when the pain occurred, I couldn't just ignore it and hope for it to go away. But I had also been through this routine multiple times only to be told that nothing was wrong.

This visit to the ER, I vowed, would be different. I told the ER doctor I would not be leaving the emergency room without an answer. Fear is one thing, but these symptoms were not in my head. Something was wrong.

The good thing about my history of pulmonary embolism is that emergency room personnel take my symptoms quite seriously. I never have to wait in the waiting room for someone to call me back—there is always a medical staff member waiting for me once I get through the check-in process to bring me straight back.

Settled in a room, the medical staff quickly checked my vitals and hooked me up to a cardiac monitor to get an EKG. Then they took my blood and sent me for a chest x-ray. And just to be extra careful, they sent me for a CT scan. Although I told the doctors that the symptoms were not the same as an embolus, they took me through the same round of tests, multiple x-rays, and scans I had been through multiple times before.

A few hours later, the ER doctor came into my room to let me know that my heart looked good and that there was no clot in my lungs. My face instantly felt hot with frustration and anger. While it is good to get such news, I was afraid that I would have to leave again with no real answers.

"I told you when I got here that this pain is different from the other times I have had an embolism," I said angrily. "There has to be something going on."

Ignoring me, the doctor moved to the scans on the wall and pointed to a large white spot in the center of my chest. He said, "It's probably time to get that mass in your chest evaluated."

My head whipped around to the monitor and the doctor. *Excuse me? Did he say what I think he just said?* I squinted at the scans hanging from the wall and looked at the spot he pointed to with the end of his pen.

"I can tell from your past scans that this mass has been growing for some time," the doctor continued. "I'd like to have a pulmonologist come and take a look."

It was at this point that the doctor made eye contact with me and, seeing my pale face and wide eyes, learned that I had not been told about a large mass in my chest that had been allowed to grow year after year. Multiple visits to the ER with chest discomfort, multiple doctors telling me nothing abnormal was found, and multiple scans clearly showing a mass growing in my chest. I'm not a doctor, but perhaps that was the cause of my discomfort.

"Are you saying there is a tumor in my chest?"

"We won't know what it is until we have it evaluated further," he continued.

I had come in ready to fight someone to get an answer, but it had never occurred to me that the answer would be a kiwi-sized mass in my chest. I didn't know yet what type of growth it was or whether it was malignant—I certainly hoped it wasn't malignant since it had been there for so long. The ER doctor referred me to a pulmonologist, who referred me to a cardiothoracic surgeon to do more tests. First, they needed to find out what the mass was and then create a plan to determine how to remove it. I had been in and out of the hospital throughout my forties with one life-threatening illness after another, and now, at forty-seven years old, I was facing my mortality once again.

It would take weeks before I could get in to have tests completed and more time to create a treatment plan. I had nothing but time to think about my life, my death, and everything in between. I began a life inventory—reviewing all I had done and all I had left to do. I also thought a lot about my belief systems. What did I truly believe?

All throughout my life, people have been picking me out of a crowd to talk to me about Jesus—to convert me to Christianity and to save my soul. A woman once stopped me in the grocery store by faking interest in something I had been looking at on the shelf and then awkwardly asked me about my belief in Jesus. When I rented a room from a couple after first moving up to Summit County, the woman I rented from would come into my room at night, sit on my bed, preach to me about the teachings of Jesus, and try to get me to believe as she did. Time and again, people have tried to "save" me. I even had a pair of teenagers approach me and my friend Lauri when we were walking to the entrance of Cheyenne Frontier Days. They told us they were doing a school project and wanted to just ask a few questions. It became clear after the first one or two questions that what they were really there for was to convince us about their Christian faith. This happened so much that I thought I might have "Heathen" written on my forehead.

Several things about these encounters bothered me. First, the people involved assumed I needed saving—never asking what my beliefs were or if I cared to be saved. Second, they assumed they had the power to save me. Why did they think they had the power to save me, but I don't possess the same? If I need to be saved, couldn't I take it upon myself to do the deed?

I hear people talk about faith all the time, and the word and idea fascinate me. There is something deeply moving about a person who has faith. Not those who claim they are religious and use that against others, but those who have true faith in what they believe. It could be a Buddhist monk, Catholic priest or nun, rabbi, imam, or the spiritual neighbor down the street. It doesn't matter. What does matter is that these people have studied and learned along the way, and they have formed a set of beliefs on that knowledge, regardless of what others think. They don't work to try to get everyone else to believe as they do, but when asked, they are kind enough to talk about their religion or beliefs and share additional knowledge.

These are the people I wish to meet. The seekers, the mystics, those who want to explore the universe and all her mysteries.

I was baptized and raised Catholic. My great-uncle was a priest, my great-aunt was a nun, and my ancestors built the first Catholic church in Wheatland, Wyoming. Coming from multiple lines of Irish families, Catholicism runs deep in our family.

Over the years, however, my beliefs have shifted. It probably started when I was enrolled in catechism classes, and I was kicked out shortly thereafter for asking too many questions. I have never been able to believe in something that cannot be questioned.

So, what do I believe? That is complicated.

I guess you could say that I am a spiritual, nonreligious seeker. I believe, but not in any one given religion or doctrine. I also believe that all religions have some truth. I once heard someone say that religion is for people who are afraid of hell, whereas spirituality is for those who have already been through hell and have come out on the other side. I felt that.

I studied what I had been taught as a child. I was taught that any perceived wrong would be met with hellfire and brimstone (think Dante's Inferno). I was taught about judgment and the need to kneel and beg for forgiveness—to worship in order to be saved. I was taught not to question authority. None of this seemed right to me. Why would God give me a brain if he didn't wish for me to use it to seek answers?

So, I studied other faiths. I went to a Mormon event with a friend just to see what it was all about. But when I learned that the event only involved women and that there was a clear separation between what women and men were allowed to do, they lost me.

As for Christianity, I had already had too many Christians call me a sinner or a heathen or, my personal favorite, "of the devil," for me to be okay with that faith.

But I also know that there is more out there than what I can see with my eyes or study scientifically. Paramedics I know have encounters all the time with things that can't be explained with science. It is something as simple as the gut feeling inside a room that tells you to be on guard or as unbelievable as the spirit of a recently deceased individual sitting next to you on the bench seat of the ambulance.

I often hear medical people say that they are not religious because they believe in science. I also hear religious people deny science if it goes against their beliefs or their faith. I am of the opinion that these two things don't have to exist separately. What if science just hasn't caught up yet to what we humans sense or see in the spirit world? I mean, science once thought the Earth was flat until more information was presented to illustrate that this understanding was wrong (Yes, people, the Earth is in fact round).

So, I remain open to all possibilities. As a medic, I saw horrific things, and I saw the most beautiful things, all because of the wonders in this world and how people respond. Each person deserves to believe how they believe based on the experiences of their life. And those who have found true faith—unwavering, unconditional faith—those are the ones I would like to get to know better. I would have loved to have one conversation with Mother Teresa. I would love to meet the Dalai Lama. I seek interactions with true believers of all faiths and backgrounds. Those who can sit and have a conversation without judgment or agenda. Those who enjoy the questions. Those who are able to smile through tragedy.

We are all created the same way and live in the same universe, but we each have a different set of experiences. Maybe we understand the spiritual world, and maybe we don't. I think that most of us have seen a glimpse—just enough to form our opinions and beliefs and just enough to judge others. And if you are a seeker who also likes philosophy, then sign me up.

I am ready to come and play.

CHAPTER 15

STORIES

Each year, a group of paramedic friends and I would travel to Custer, South Dakota, to camp for several days and then go to the Crazy Horse Walk, a once-a-year fundraiser where we could walk up to the Crazy Horse memorial and walk on his arm, all while supporting the ongoing construction of the site.

On one of these trips, I carpooled with my friend Lauri, and I brought my German shepherd, Sulley. I had a topper on the back of the truck so Sulley could hang out in back and still occasionally stick his head through the window into the cab as we headed north out of Colorado into Wyoming and then South Dakota.

Approximately ten miles from our campsite, right around dusk, a deer ran from the side of the road directly in front of my truck. As I slammed on the brakes, we hit the animal head-on. The deer's body went into my engine compartment and up onto the hood. Luckily, the windshield was not broken, and we were uninjured. Even Sulley fared well in the accident without any consequences.

Unfortunately, the vehicle was rendered immobile, and we happened to be in one area of the road without any cellular service. Lauri and I stood in front of the truck, trying to get service to call a tow truck, while our other friends all drove past our vehicle without seeing us or stopping.

Seriously, I knew my powers of invisibility were strong, but I didn't think they were that strong.

Finally, after about fifteen minutes, a minivan pulled over to the side of the road with a family inside. The driver got out of the vehicle and took a look at my wrecked truck with the dead deer attached.

"Are you both okay?" he asked.

"Yes," I said. "We aren't injured, but we need a tow truck, and we don't have any cell reception."

The man and my friend Lauri both went up the hill to try to get a signal to call out of the area. I stayed behind in case anyone else came along who might be able to help.

I smiled at the woman in the minivan sitting in the passenger seat. Her kids were in the back, staring at me. She rolled down her window and leaned out to speak with me, elbows and arms on the door. I was ready for some small talk until we were able to get help, so I took a step forward and smiled.

"Have you accepted the Lord Jesus Christ as your personal savior?"

Taken aback, I paused before answering. "Umm, no."

"I'd like to talk to you about Jesus and how he can become an important, if not the most important person in your life," she went on, seemingly thrilled to have an audience. Her husband was a pastor, and she helped in his ministry. I was literally trapped on the side of the road with my freaked-out dog, a busted vehicle, and a deer carcass in my truck's engine compartment, and that seemed to be the opportune time to save me from my heathen ways (I told you—it happens to me all the time).

I conversed with her for a while until Lauri and the pastor returned. He told us he would call for a tow truck once he got into town. We both thanked them, and the family went on their way while Lauri and I returned to the cab of my truck to wait.

As we sat there, I told Lauri about how the woman had tried to save my poor soul on the side of the road. Lauri considered herself a recovering Catholic, so we had a bit of fun with the experience. We laughed about the absurdity of people trying to convert complete strangers. The laughing led to more jokes about religion, which led to much more laughing.

With each minute that passed and each joke we told, the weather turned more ominous. As time passed, the sky got dark, and it started to rain. The more we laughed, the harder it rained until the rain turned to hail pelting my already-injured truck.

Sulley, the big beautiful 120-pound monster in the back of the truck, squeezed his body through the small window into the cab, sat on Lauri's lap, and trembled with fright at the noise caused by pounding hail on the roof.

"Perhaps we shouldn't have been making fun of the nice Christian lady," I said, laughing. "It seems we have upset God."

More hilarity ensued.

The storm didn't last long, and by the time it cleared up, a tow truck pulled over in front of us. The driver got out and examined my vehicle. After introducing himself, he shook my hand. Then, just in case the day hadn't been weird enough, he leaned in toward me and said, "Is this your first kill?"

I could practically hear the *Deliverance* music playing in the background.

"Yes," I said. "It's my first kill."

"If you want, I can get you a souvenir—maybe an eye or something?"

He pointed toward his truck, ready to spring into action.

"Ummm, no, I'm good, thanks."

Our adventures added some fun to the conversation around the campfire later that night as we arrived safely at our campsite and sat among friends.

I LOVE STORIES. Happy, sad, inspirational, or tragic. Those times around the campfire with my paramedic family are some of my best memories. George is the best storyteller I have ever known. He would keep me laughing for hours. Stories are how you really get to understand the world.

When I traveled around Europe after paramedic school, I picked up the book, *On the Road* by Jack Kerouac. Prior to this time, I didn't read much outside of school, but I thought I would read this book specifically because I was, in fact, on the road. I ended up finishing it and reading twelve more in the six weeks I traveled.

Ever since that time, I have had at least two books with me at all times—fiction, nonfiction, biography, historical, horror, you name it. If I see someone reading a book on the bus or a train, I write down the title and add it to my list of books to read.

I just love diving into a good story. And there is nothing quite like the epics—the love, the loss, the tragedy, and the triumph. When I finished reading *Lord of the Rings*, bawling my eyes out, I immediately turned back to page one and started the story over again because I just didn't want it to end. The small hobbit and his friends overcoming insurmountable odds to beat the evil forces that are taking over the world. One small person making a huge difference. It's tragedy and beauty, all wrapped together.

Man, I love that!

I especially like the stories that show humans as the flawed, irrational, unpredictable people we are—where darkness and light are mixed, and our circumstances and choices are the determining factors in whether we commit good or evil deeds. Yin and yang.

In my twenties I was an idealist. I believed in the very best of all people. I believed that anyone could be redeemed. I believed that good would always conquer evil. Then, I became a paramedic. In emergency services, you are forced to be a part of someone's worst day. Sometimes that worst day is the heart attack of a beloved family member. But other times, it is taking someone to the hospital who was injured while murdering a family member. During my time working as a detox counselor, I had to intake a convicted pedophile who talked to me about his crimes. I had to show compassion to someone who had done unspeakable things to a child.

I found cynicism while working as a paramedic. My idealism started to crack and later shatter. Instead of looking at the world through rose-colored glasses, I started to see everyone as a threat or a future disappointment. I already had a host of trust and fear issues, so this was a really bad combination. And when I started thinking *just suck it up* when treating someone with a femur fracture, it was probably time to exit stage left. It was a clear sign to me that if I stayed a paramedic long-term, it would irrevocably change who I was—and I wasn't ready to go to the dark side.

This was one of the reasons why I looked to emergency management as a second career. It would still allow me to be a healer and a public servant helping during a disaster, but I would also be one step removed from the scene. Surprisingly, the field of emergency management restored my faith in humanity.

I know now that while working as a paramedic, I saw people who did both evil and beautiful things. Every day. And this was amplified exponentially working in disaster work. Communities come together and help one another. Perfect strangers donate goods or services just because they can. It is through the actions of each individual that we get through this thing called life.

How many small actions happen every single day—random acts that seem small and sometimes insignificant but that ultimately have a huge impact? It could be that one kid that says something nice to another kid having a bad day that ultimately keeps the kid from harming himself. It could be a nurse who holds someone's hand as they take their last breath, ensuring they know they are not alone. It could be that extra time that an officer takes with a scared family member or even just a compliment at just the right time.

I know now that there is no such thing as a good person or a bad person. Instead, we are all shades of gray. It is our choices that lead us to one side or the other. Every single person is both a hero and a deeply flawed individual. Each day we are tested and given a chance to start fresh, to right wrongs from the past, to possibly be the hero in someone's story.

Very few of us truly think about how all our actions and inactions are interconnected. But anyone who reads, especially the epics, understands that each person—no matter how small—has an integral part to play in the stories of the lives of people around them. When I think of this, I hope to make the choices that will lead myself and everyone I encounter to the light instead of the darkness.

CHAPTER 16

Confidence

"ALL RIGHT, EVERYONE. We are going to get this briefing started."

The incident management team members quieted and looked to the front of the room. I was a Planning Section Chief trainee with a Type 1 IMT, and it was my first briefing with the team. As the plans chief, I ran the briefing.

"The objectives for today's operational period include: 1) Providing for the safety and security of incident personnel in the execution of all incident operations by discussing and adhering to the ten standard firefighting orders and the eighteen watch out situations; 2) Providing for the protection of all infrastructure and improvements while considering firefighter and public safety first; and 3) Maintaining good communications with Incident Command and Operations."

Following this, I went over the current fire situation and then turned it over to the Operations section chief to go over the day's operation. While the Ops chief was talking, I noticed a few people in the back of the room talking to one another. Heads turned around occasionally, and I knew that the side conversation was causing a distraction to the briefing. I also knew that it was up to me, as the Plans chief, to control the briefing. But I was also a trainee, so I hesitated.

As the briefing continued, the conversation in the back continued. When it was my turn to talk again, I asked that all side conversations cease before having the incident meteorologist go over the day's weather. But as I looked to the back of the room, I noticed that two men continued talking.

"The two of you in the back," I said loudly to get their attention. "If you cannot be quiet during the briefing, I need to ask you to leave."

For the first time since the briefing began, there was complete silence. A bunch of stunned faces looked between me and the two men in the back of the room. One of them grinned, apologized, and quieted for the remainder of the briefing.

Once the briefing ended, I felt a slap on my back and laughter from a few of the team members. The planning chief for the team, who I was training under, came up to me and said, "I can't believe you just told the incident commander that if he couldn't behave, he had to leave the briefing."

I started to explain why I did it, but he cut me off. "I am not saying you were wrong. That was awesome! You are going to be a great planning chief. You need to be the bad guy in the room, keep people on schedule, and run your briefings efficiently." He doubled up in laughter, "If you have the balls to kick out the incident commander, you have the right personality for this job."

Others came up to me after the briefing, either shaking their heads or laughing. I am sure that a few of them had wished at some point to put the incident commander in his place, so the majority of folks showed some admiration on their faces as they filed out for the day.

"You know," the Plans chief continued, "in order to be great at this job, you have to be a bit of an asshole." He patted my shoulder. "And you are going to be great at this job."

I thought about it for a minute. "You do realize you just called me an asshole, right?"

He walked away with a grin on his face.

When I first became a paramedic, I regularly worked with another medic named Matt. Since we were both paramedics, we would alternate between providing patient care and driving. Early in my career, when we entered a room or building with a patient everyone would automatically look to Matt to give him a report. This became an annoyance for me.

"What the hell, Matt?" I said after one call. "The firefighters always give you reports, and the patients always look to you for guidance." I wasn't irritated at Matt. He hadn't done anything to cause this, but the situation was irritating, nonetheless. "Why does everyone just assume you are in charge?"

He gestured up and down with his hand at my stance and general appearance. "People look at both of us, and they assume I am in charge because you don't look like you are in charge. If you want that to change, you need to change."

Well la de da, Matt. I asked for the truth, and I got it.

I thought about his advice a lot following that conversation. I harnessed my watcher nature and began to watch people on emergency scenes, specifically those in leadership roles or those with natural presence. I could tell when someone lacked confidence. I could tell when people were naturally drawn to a leader on scene. I picked up on the subtle signs from every interaction and began to learn what would be needed to change.

I actively worked to create a more confident tone in my work. I had to learn how to take all my insecurities and fears and bury them. I tried different things on different calls to see what success looked like. I learned from every single person I encountered.

Some say that people are born with command presence and that it cannot be taught. But I am here to say that this idea is wrong. Less than a year after my conversation with Matt, the tables had turned. I noticed that whenever we arrived on scene, the firefighters and patients would routinely look to me for answers. It became so prevalent that Matt even noticed and complained to me about it. I had taken a weakness and made it my strength.

The place I first learned confidence, however, was around a pool table. While living in Las Vegas in my early twenties, I began playing pool. I joined a few pool leagues at a bar called the Rum Runner near my home and became a regular fixture there—not to drink, but to play pool. I stopped by every night and would play anyone who wished to play.

Over time, I learned that an eighty-year-old man would come by every Saturday and give free lessons to anyone willing to listen and learn. My response? Sign me up, please! I showed up religiously to learn from him, and my game improved dramatically. I later learned that this man had once been a world champion pool player, but in that bar on those Saturdays, he was, to me, just a man willing to take the time with a younger person to pass along the lessons he had learned along the way.

By the time I left Las Vegas and headed back to Colorado to begin my career, I had become an excellent pool player. I played regularly in tournaments, played in leagues multiple nights a week, and I started to win a lot of money by playing the game. What I loved about Las Vegas is that it never mattered who you played—everyone thought everyone else was hustling them, so people always played to win. I believe this is why my game became so good. I was constantly tested. I lost a lot. But with each loss, I learned something new—and I really liked the challenge.

When I moved to Colorado, I got a front office administrative job at an ophthalmologist's office and continued to play pool occasionally once I got settled. As part of my new job, we would travel up to Glenwood Springs one week a month to provide eye care to patients in the area. On one of these early trips, I brought my pool cue, and after work, I went to a bar called Doc Holliday's to play a few games.

I entered the bar and moved to the back of the room, where a pool table stood. A few college guys were playing a game, and the saloon had quite a few people at the bar milling around drinking. I set my pool cue carrying case down next to a booth and then reached into my pocket for some quarters, which I always had on me, and set them down on the table to play the next available game. Then, I sat down to wait and watch the game currently underway.

A young college kid picked up the quarters I had just set on the table and walked over to my seat. "We are playing for money on this table, honey." He held out his hand to give me back my coins.

Unfazed, I merely shrugged and said, "No problem. I'll play for money."

"No, I don't think you understand," he said, persisting. "This is a serious pool game. You don't want to lose your money, so you may want to play somewhere else, honey."

Honey. Grrrr.

If he had been a smart man, he would have noticed that I had walked in carrying my own cue, meaning that I probably had some experience around a pool table. He also decided to argue with me about whether I should play when I clearly was all right with betting on pool.

I had never encountered this in Las Vegas. There, it was assumed that if you were playing, you were a player. No one ever gave me a break in any game or treated me any differently than any other player. A five-year-old could have approached a table in Vegas and no one would have blinked or let down their guard while playing. It was always an even competition, and I loved it. This was the first time I had ever been judged as "less than" while attempting to play a game of pool.

I did not like the feeling.

With every argument, my irritation blossomed and quickly turned to anger. Luckily for me, my game dramatically improved once I became angry.

"How about we play for twenty bucks?" I said, slamming a twenty-dollar bill on the table, finally fed up. "And to make it a fair game, I'll play left-handed."

For a moment, he was speechless. Then, looking around the table and noticing that he was now being watched by several people in the bar, he straightened up and got his swagger back. "Fine," he snarled. "And I'll play left-handed as well."

Awareness of your surroundings and your competition is a requirement if you plan to compete and win. This college kid, assuming I had no idea what I was doing, had first tried to shame me into leaving and then made a foolish bet with an unknown player. For one, he had not seen me play. Had he taken that time, he may have made a different decision. Second, he would have noticed that I am actually left-handed. I had not placed myself in a weak position at all. It was the first time I ever hustled someone playing pool, and I am happy to say that I kicked his little ass all over that table.

At the end of the game, I went to shake his hand, but instead, he threw his cue on the ground and turned around to storm out without paying the twenty dollars he owed me. Before he could get more than a few feet, however, several people in the bar stopped him and started yelling at him to pay up. He had made such a fuss about playing me and then let his anger get the best of him. I wasn't fazed by his outburst or reaction and really just wanted him to leave so I could play pool in peace, but the patrons of the bar had other plans. They blocked his path and heckled him, yelling until he finally turned around and threw a twenty-dollar bill on the table. Everyone in the bar cheered.

The rest of the night, people came and went, but no one that put a quarter on the table did so without understanding that I knew the game and played for keeps.

Paramedic school was one of the worst years of my life. Learning paramedicine is hard enough as it is, and most find the year to be unbearably stressful, but I was also dealing with my father, whose alcoholism had reached an unbearable low. And I was dealing with an instructor who wanted me to fail.

The year started off okay, but as in other occasions in my life, one of my instructors found me to be too opinionated. I asked too many questions, and I just didn't fit into the box I was supposed to fit into. You see, I was raised by a strong woman who was also raised by a strong woman who was raised by a strong woman. Every woman in my mother's line was a trailblazer, someone who did not take no for an answer and went out and conquered the world without waiting for permission from anyone. It is in my DNA.

I am a pain in the ass.

I know this. I accept this.

I have tried the patience of many authority figures throughout the years. In sixth grade, my teacher threw a tape dispenser at me, she was so frustrated. I ducked and then quickly said, "You really shouldn't throw things at your students; you could hurt someone." She was so angry she had to leave the room.

In junior high, I was kicked out of catechism because I asked the priest too many questions—if he could have answered the questions, it wouldn't have been a problem, but I think I outlined the absurdity of some of the teachings when they could not find rational answers to a twelve-year old's questions.

In high school, I told my music instructor to fuck off after he made a rude comment about how well I was "filling out" my uniform. He promptly scolded me, called me into his office, and called my mother. After telling her what I had done, my mother asked to speak with me. At that point, I outlined in detail what he had said to me. She proceeded to give him the thrashing he so rightly deserved (like I said before, I did not come from a line of meek women).

So, it did not really come as a surprise to me that one of my paramedic instructors disliked me and tried to keep me in my place. He put up several additional barriers to my success, adding to an already stressful time. It wasn't the first time I ran into barriers, and it would not be the last. I felt as if I were swimming upstream in quicksand—one problem after the other. But my entry into emergency management changed everything.

When I applied for my first full-time position as an emergency manager in Park County, Colorado, I met with the Board of Commissioners as part of the interview process. During that interview, I deviated from what I would typically do in that situation. When they asked if I had anything to add or if I had any questions, I leaned in and said, "If you hire me, I will be an excellent emergency manager. I was born for this work, and I am excited for this opportunity. If you hire me, you won't regret it."

Now, this could have gone two ways. The first is that I could have come off as arrogant, and I could have repelled the board and lost the opportunity. The other is that they would see my excitement and determination and decide to hire me. Luckily, it was the latter.

After being hired, I met with Jim Gardner, one of the county commissioners who ultimately hired me. He was an incredibly kind man who looked like he had come straight out of the gold mines of the 1800s. He had a long salt-and-pepper beard, always wore suspenders, and always had a laugh to share with those around him. While we talked that day, he told me that the minute he met me, he knew I had a fire in my belly, and he knew that that fire would cause me to do good things. He told me that was why they hired me—the fact that I was made of fire.

It was one of the first times in my life where my fiery nature wasn't seen as a weakness or something to overcome. My fire is what got me into the field of emergency management, and since that day and that conversation with Jim, I have never doubted that my fire would take me anywhere I wish to go.

Many will try to diminish a fire in another if they perceive it as a threat, and many will actively work to destroy someone who doesn't bow down to authority. People have often tried to diminish me—to take some of my fire. Sometimes, I have to let them. But as I get older, those times are less and less. I now welcome the fire that makes me who I am, and I take the lesson Jim Gardner gave me—to use that fire to do good work.

In the words of Dr. Thomas from Grey's Anatomy, "You have greatness in you. Don't disappoint."

CHAPTER 17

WOMEN

My most memorable call was a terminally ill cancer patient whose only wish in the world was to make it to Denver so she could see and talk to her children one more time. There wasn't much that needed to be done for the patient other than comfort care, but it was that two-hour drive to Denver with just the two of us in the back of the ambulance that springs up in my mind at the rarest of moments. I remember thinking that those would most likely be her last moments and that I had better make it good.

We talked about random things, including her life and her illness. But most of all, we talked about her children. At the beginning of the trip, she was anxious and afraid she wouldn't live through the two-hour drive to the city. But by the end, she was calm and smiling from the memories of her children and family.

My patient made it to Denver, and she was able to spend a bit of time with her kids before her death. I didn't do much for her as a medic, but I still remember our conversation and hope it made a difference to her on her last day.

When I was a young child, my mother and I were driving home late at night on back country roads. I remember the night being especially dark. While traveling on a dirt road, my mother suddenly slammed on the brakes. Looking out the front window, I couldn't see anything lit up by the headlights that was in our way, anything that could harm us, but as I turned my head left to the driver's side to ask my mom what was wrong, I saw out her window the underside of a vehicle not two feet from our car. This was the first time I had come upon an accident in my short life, and it terrified me.

My mom quickly took off her seatbelt, looked at me and said, "I'll be right back. Stay in the car."

I grabbed her arm and asked her not to go, fear laced in my voice. For some reason, the sight of the undercarriage of the vehicle next to us made me tremble. I thought my mom wouldn't come back.

She looked at me and said, "There are people in that vehicle who may need help," and then left the car to see what happened.

I am not certain if this is the reason I chose a career as a helper, but I do think that this particular night stuck with me for a reason. I could go out there and help others or I could stay quiet and afraid.

Later, when I was an EMT working at Keystone Ski Resort, I decided to go to paramedic school. This had been my goal since attending my first EMT class and I was so excited to begin. Rick, my boss at the time, couldn't understand why I wanted to take that next step from EMT to paramedic. One day, he asked me why I wanted to go to paramedic school. He said, "You are going to have so much more responsibility, doesn't that stress you out?" In his mind, being an EMT was easier because you didn't have all the extra pressure of being the one in charge on a scene. My fear was actually the opposite. As an EMT, I had some knowledge, but what if I were in a position where someone needed my help and I couldn't help them because I never learned how? What if I allowed my fear to hold me back? I told him that I would much rather have the skills to help when needed than not be in a position to help when needed.

The stress of knowing someone is in harm's way without the ability to assist was more stressful to me than anything else. And every time I felt a bit of pressure or fear, I would recall my mom running out to help a total stranger on a dark back road without hesitation. I didn't want to be the child hiding in fear in the car, wondering what bad thing is going to happen. I wanted to be the person running to help just in case someone needs a hand.

I joined a male-dominated profession, but due to my past I never really thought about it much. I had always been around mostly boys and men. Most of my young tomboy life was spent with my two brothers and with my male friends. I played the drums on an all-male snare line, and I was doing search and rescue every weekend with mostly boys and men.

It wasn't until I became a paramedic that I began to see the true power in women and my relationships with women. Some of the toughest, kindest, compassionate, kick-ass women I have ever met were in the fire service and on the ambulance with me as a paramedic. They were always there for me when I had a bad call, or needed advice, or just needed help finding my dog. We camped together, we went to concerts, we worked hard, we traveled, we faced the same traumas, and we laughed harder than I ever have before. This was the first time in my life I truly understood the power and strength of women who support one another.

When I was a little girl, my mother told me that there was nothing I could not accomplish if I put my mind to it, and she told me to always dream big. Few things you hear stick with you forever, and often the things that do stick are the negative comments that shape us. But this one thing stuck with me throughout my life. Every time I was told I could not do something, my first response was, "The hell I can't!"

I was told I would never be on the snare line in the high school drumline because girls were not allowed. I said, "Watch me," and by my senior year, I was on that snare line. I was told by a group of Denver firefighters that I did not belong in the field. I said, "The hell I don't," and I became successful as a firefighter and a paramedic. I was told time and again that there were things I could not do or should not do, but time and again, I proved my critics wrong.

My father taught me fear. My mom taught me courage.

While my father became a cautionary tale and a lesson in excess, my mother became my compass. She was able to guide me in my youth while also giving me room to make my own decisions and grow to be my own person. She provided encouragement while also providing critique to keep me from great harm. She stayed with my dad long after she knew her marriage to him was over but was smart enough to leave the minute she knew that her children would be okay.

None of this was by accident. Her mother was also a force of nature, as well as her mother before her and on and on through our genealogy. My great-grandmother was called "The Little Mother of the Prairie" since she was a midwife and healer whom people called upon when in trouble. My grandmother was a World War II nurse and, after the war, became a public health nurse—a job she had her entire life. My mother followed in her footsteps and became a nurse and epidemiologist, later teaching the next generation of nurses. Each of these women broke barriers within their time and never let the dictates of society tell them what they could and could not do. They also were all healers.

My mother had tried to tell me several times when I was younger that I should become a paramedic or a firefighter, but I always thought she was nuts. For me, it didn't seem obvious until I was stopped at that stoplight in Las Vegas, contemplating my life, when that ambulance drove by. After that, the path was clear, and I realized that everything I had been trained for and everything I had gone through as a child had led up to a career helping people. I also realized that it was a calling—possibly one that was deeply ingrained in my DNA from centuries of women who had been healers and who had broken barriers in their time.

One such woman was my great-aunt Bea. She was a seamstress in Chicago and took my great-grandmother in when she was a young woman starting school. Aunt Bea was a successful single woman in the late 1800s, living at a time when women did not have much value outside of marriage. She chose her own path in life and was successful as a businesswoman and entrepreneur. She chose not to let people dictate her value or what was the "right path" and created something that was right for her.

I connect with my great-aunt Bea more than any other woman in my family. Like Aunt Bea, I wanted to blaze my own path and determine my own destiny. When younger, I would tell people I didn't want to get married or have children, and the response was often, "Don't worry, there's still time," or "You'll change your mind when you're older."

Nope. Never changed my mind.

At a family lunch, my cousin decided to tell me about how empty my life must be without children.

"There is so much love between a mother and child," she said, holding her infant son. "I just think that you are missing out on so much by not having kids."

"Not everyone was born to be a parent," I said, trying hard to mask my annoyance.

"You just don't know what you are missing," she continued. "Can you truly tell me that you never want to get married and have a family?"

I gestured around the large table. "I have a family."

"You know what I mean." She went on to tell me how I couldn't possibly be as happy as she was with her husband and children.

Meanwhile, her infant son grabbed a large handful of spaghetti and then grabbed onto my cousin's blond hair. He was fidgeting and fussing and grabbing anything he could reach, all while spreading the spaghetti all over her shirt and hair.

"You really aren't selling the whole motherhood thing right now," I said, watching the spaghetti noodles drip from her blond hair.

I smiled at her son.

Finally, giving up on me, my cousin looked over to my mother, who sat at the end of the table near both of us. "Barb," she said, "tell Lori how great it was to be a mother."

Without missing a beat, my mom said, "Actually, I never really wanted to have children."

End of argument.

I smiled at my mom, silently thanking her for always having my back. And I am grateful to all of the women I have met in emergency services, especially the fabulous women from Summit County Ambulance Service who, to this day, I could call with a problem and they would lend an ear or lend a hand. You hear a lot about how women don't support one another, but I have seen another way. Perhaps it is the type of work or the stress of the job, but these women were tough as nails and sweet as pie all rolled into one. The very best of us.

CHAPTER 18

Ripples

On March 16, 2004, I started the day with a stomachache. It began as a few butterflies flying around in my belly, a specific type of anxiety or weirdness in my body that I had come to recognize well. As the day progressed, the anxiety grew, leading to chest discomfort and an entire swarm of butterflies jostling for room in my stomach and chest.

This feeling wasn't new. I recognized it from previous events. I knew that the discomfort would steadily grow until we received the call about someone dying. Call it what you will—intuition, women's instinct, hoodoo, witchcraft—but it's real and extremely accurate in its predictions of future harm.

On this day, I knew this wouldn't be the average death—something bigger was about to happen. I went out to the garage, climbed in the back of the ambulance, inspected all the equipment, and prepared everything for the unknown call that I knew would come that evening. I even set out the intubation kit, thinking I might need it later.

When this anxiety had occurred in the past, I never knew what was about to happen or to whom it might happen. The only thing I knew was that sometime soon, someone would die. I never really talked to my partners about this phenomenon—I didn't truly understand it, so I didn't expect others to either. This time the feeling was much more intense, almost debilitating uneasiness, so I broke my silence and told my partner something bad was coming, and soon someone would die. He gave me a sideways glance, a grin, and a dismissive chuckle.

About a half-hour after going to bed, we got the page. An on-duty firefighter had been found in the weight room unconscious and not breathing. Being the closest ambulance, only a mile away from the fire station, we were paged to respond. All my day's uneasiness finally made sense. It was because it wasn't a stranger that had died but a firefighter we both knew named Barry.

We arrived on scene quickly, all uneasiness now gone, and we entered the fire station to find multiple firefighters crammed in the weight room looking at the body on the floor. I reminded myself that it was more important than ever to be calm and collected at this specific scene. I worked with all these men and women, and it was their friend lying on the ground while a firefighter performed CPR.

My partner moved to Barry's head to check breathing and secure an airway while I went to work on getting a line for medications. Many of the firefighters were obviously in shock and just stood there staring as we worked. One, who stood off to the side, kept encouraging Barry to live.

"Come on, Barry," he would say. "You can do it. Fight, Barry, fight."

Another firefighter standing behind me kept quietly saying, "Good job," whenever I did something to try to help Barry.

I slid the catheter into his vein. "Good job."

I gave medications. "Good job."

I pushed fluids. "Good job."

We worked for several minutes, loaded Barry into the ambulance, and ran emergent to the medical center. We did everything we could do to save his life, but it was to no avail. Barry died in the firehouse he loved. He was fifty-six years old.

Just after finishing writing about this memory, I received a phone call from a friend of mine who worked with me when I was a paramedic in Summit County. Kim and I have kept in touch over the years and call one another a few times each year to catch up. On this occasion, however, she called with terrible news. Another paramedic friend of ours had woken up that morning and found her young daughter dead in her home.

It was strange to finish writing about a memory where a death had rocked the emergency services community only to have another just begin with a simple phone call. I am no longer part of that community and haven't been in years, but I imagined how the ripples of trauma would begin to spread. Each phone call would lead to another until everyone in the system had been notified. They would rally around Jill and Peter, who had just lost someone terribly precious to them and to each of us who knew her. We had all watched Maddie grow up over the years, and we participated in many of the events that would ultimately shape her early life.

And although most of the people I worked with in Summit County were not classified as a traditional family, the bonds that were made during those years together were and are still strong. When one person suffers a trauma, it affects the entire system, like ripples in a pond spreading out all around you.

It has been many years since I resigned as a paramedic and started a new career in emergency management, but I still consider myself a burned-out medic. When thinking about my time as a medic, I mostly remember the nights in the freezing cold, calf-deep in mud or slush, working to save a life while also trying to keep my latex gloves from freezing to my hands. I remember the drunks: the guy who passed out in a snow drift only to have a snowplow come along and bury him on the side of the road, the dueling pukers I had in the back of the ambulance on New Year's Eve, and the multiple drunk drivers who caused carnage on the highways, sometimes killing people and not even knowing it. I even had one drunk patient call 911 at

2 a.m. for an ambulance to respond to the bar because he felt dizzy after drinking. Dizzy after drinking—really? I wanted to grab him by the ankles and tip him over the railing of the balcony where he was standing just so we would have a real emergency.

The moments that will stick with me forever, however, were those times when I made a difference to someone in the smallest of ways. It wasn't the big call, with people everywhere, lights flashing, and multiple victims needing help. It was the time when I was able to comfort a scared little child or when I got the chance to save a dog's life after its owner died in a car accident. Most importantly, for paramedics, it is those moments when you meet someone who sticks with you forever, either through the words they say or the things they do.

I remember vividly, and still have pictures, of Maddie helping us during an exercise at the age of fifteen. She had agreed to be moulaged for the event. She wore old clothes that she didn't mind getting ruined and invited her friends to join her. We provided the makeup needed to fake several injuries to make the exercise as realistic as possible—a broken bone here, a laceration there. Maddie chose the most gruesome of injuries, with a gaping head wound and a prosthetic eyeball hanging from her left eyelid. She refused to let us remove the makeup after the exercise and instead decided there was no better time than that moment to go with her friends to Walmart to do a bit of shopping.

That was Maddie.

Those are the memories I have that make me smile or laugh as I think of the things I loved about being a paramedic. My absolute best memories involve the crews and the camaraderie of the people assigned to each shift. It is the memories of the people I met along the way—the other firefighters, EMTs, and paramedics that were always willing to rally in times of need.

While the worst days are memorable because of the families of the deceased or the amount of work involved in trying to save someone, for me, they are more memorable because of what followed at crew headquarters to relieve the stress of the day. These are the moments I miss most about being a paramedic.

I miss my extended family.

CHAPTER 19

HUMOR

On a cold winter day in January, two coworkers of mine, Ed and Dave, had a transport from Summit Medical Center to St. Anthony's Central Hospital in Denver. The time of transport is typically around one and a half hours, but with bad weather, it could be as much as four hours. This was a bad day. Not only had the snow begun to fall, but it was around 3 p.m., right when skier traffic from the mountains was at its worst. They were in bumper-to-bumper traffic, and it was looking like an exceptionally long trip. Ed was in the back, tending to the patient, while Dave drove the ambulance.

Dave was an older gentleman who had worked as an EMT at the ambulance service for many years. Because of his age, or maybe because of years of listening to the siren, he was a little hard of hearing. But he was also a rather good guy, always willing to assist when needed. Ed was younger, a paramedic, and a little cocky. I know what you are thinking. "What? A paramedic with an ego? That never happens." But Ed gave the old paramedic stereotype of arrogance a run for its money. Like Dave, however, Ed was a good person, and he was also a good paramedic.

As Ed tended to the patient in the back of the ambulance, he noticed that a car was following them too closely. This is a dangerous situation in an ambulance since it is really just a cab with a hollow box behind it. Anyone who hits the back of an ambulance has a good chance of going through the patient compartment. Close drivers are irritating to medics when tending to patients because it creates a dangerous situation for both the crew and the patient.

This situation irritated Ed.

So, while the ambulance was stopped in traffic on that cold winter day, Ed decided he was going to lay down the law to that driver. Now, most of us would just get on the radio and call to have the State Patrol come and remove that person from our bumper so that we can move along safely on our merry way. But not Ed. Instead, he leaned forward into the space between the patient compartment and the cab and told Dave he would be right back. He then proceeded to open the side compartment door and leave the ambulance.

First, you never leave a patient unattended. It just isn't done. And second, Ed forgot an important piece of information. Dave is hard of hearing. He didn't hear Ed say he was leaving the ambulance, and he didn't hear the door open and close in the back.

So, while Ed was outside in the snow, reading the riot act to the driver behind the ambulance, the traffic eased, and Dave took his foot off the brakes and merrily pulled away. Miraculously, the traffic cleared so that the ambulance could gain some speed, putting some distance between Ed—haughtily lecturing some unsuspecting fool—and his patient in the back of the ambulance. For someone with an ego as big as Ed's, this had to be a terribly embarrassing situation. But more importantly, he was now stuck in the middle of an icy interstate without a ride.

Luckily for Ed, though, we used Nextel phones at the time, meaning that he could contact Dave by direct connect (like a walkie-talkie) and get him to stop. Ed started running after the ambulance while he attempted to contact his partner.

"Dave, stop the ambulance!"

Dave picked up the phone. "Who is this?"

"It's Ed. Stop the ambulance."

"Ed is tending to a patient right now. Can I have him call you back?"

"Dave, this *is* Ed! I'm no longer in the ambulance. Stop the vehicle!"

Dave, frustrated by this caller, finally leaned over and swung his arm toward the patient compartment, holding the phone in his hand. "Hey, Ed. There's someone on the phone for you."

There was a short pause. Then the patient, who was luckily conscious and alert, said, "Dude, that guy's not back here anymore."

This Dave heard clearly.

My boss told me this story while I was driving back from Denver. I had to pull over. Never in my life had I laughed so hard. I laughed so hard I honestly thought I was going to pass out from a lack of air. Tears flowed out of my eyes so fast I couldn't see, and just as the black spots began swimming in my vision, I inhaled deeply and began wheezing with an occasional snort for good measure.

To this day, I giggle like a little girl just thinking about Ed running down I-70, Dave obliviously driving away, and a patient lying on a gurney in the back of the ambulance, wondering what the hell was going on.

I MENTIONED THAT I have a sick sense of humor. This has always been true, but I honed this skill as an emergency responder. You see, the secret is that the only people who make it in the field of emergency services are those with a sick sense of humor. Without it, you cannot survive.

When responding to the most difficult of calls, we use humor to cut through the stress. We also spent inordinate amounts of time with one another, so the typical workplace etiquette that exists between colleagues only lasted through your first shift with a new partner.

After that, you got to know a whole lot about your crewmates or partners. You slept in the same quarters and cooked meals together. It is impossible to keep up a facade in that environment.

As crews got more comfortable with one another, they also became more like siblings. This ultimately would lead to elaborate pranks or inappropriate humor. The more stressful the shift, the more inappropriate the prank or the humor. Even our boss wasn't immune. He walked into his office one day to find a life-sized Kermit the Frog sitting in his chair, slumped over his desk, with a sombrero on his head, pills covering his desk, and a bottle of whiskey in his hand.

We practiced several activities to decrease the stress. This could include drag racing the ambulances down Highway 9 in the middle of the night or mooning people out the passenger window of the ambulance on Colfax Avenue after dropping off a patient in Denver.

A long-running prank involving almost everyone in the ambulance service employed an old ratty couch. It sat outside one of the ambulance bays for a long time, and someone must have decided to take matters into their own hands. The couch first showed up outside a fellow paramedic's house, sitting on the lawn as if it belonged there. A few days later, it showed up at another employee's house. From there, it mysteriously made the rounds to multiple people who worked on the ambulance service, sometimes hanging from a balcony, other times on top of their vehicle. This occurred for over a year, and you never knew if you would be next.

My favorite of all pranks, which also happened quite frequently, involved entering the ambulance bay and hearing the soft singing of the *Mission Impossible* theme song. This inevitably meant that several crew members were hiding in the bay, biding their time, waiting for a crewmember to come along and be hit by a stream of water from the multiple super-soakers charged and ready. To this day, the *Mission Impossible* theme song brings a smile to my face. It also causes me to duck and cover.

CHAPTER 20

Coping

MY PATIENT, A fifty-five-year-old man in apparent good health, had come to the 2003 Keystone Ski Resort Fourth of July Festival with his family. While walking around the vendors and food tents, he began to feel chest pain. He also saw the fire engine parked nearby, so he veered toward it and did his best to reach the responders. Just before reaching the fire engine, he collapsed.

Our ambulance was across the street at the time of the call, so it took us just a few minutes to get on scene. When my partner and I arrived, the patient was no longer breathing and had no pulse. Fire personnel had begun CPR.

Looking down at the man, I recognized the purple hue of his face, a telltale sign of cardiac death. I knew we weren't going to bring the patient back. Many people who collapse near emergency responders, or a defibrillator, have a much better chance of survival because interventions occur immediately. We can shock the heart before we see too much damage. But then there are those patients where you know they are dead and not coming back just by looking at their faces. He was one of those. The purple hue of his face told me he was dead before he ever hit the ground. But as always, we did everything possible to bring him back.

I mentioned that the man collapsed next to the fire engine. What I didn't mention is that he also collapsed right next to the orchestra tent, which was just finishing their warm-up, preparing to start the show. We were on the back side of the tent, opposite the opening, so none of the people in the tent knew that several emergency responders were just outside, hunched over a man, performing CPR. So, shortly after we arrived and started our work, the orchestra began playing patriotic songs typical for the Fourth of July.

If you have ever had to perform CPR, you know how difficult it is to continue at a good fast pace. But even more difficult is to perform effective CPR to a beat that is different from the loud music blaring in your ear.

"Come on, man," I said for the fifth time to the firefighter doing compressions, "you need to go faster."

"I'm trying," he said, speeding up a bit, only to slow back down to the beat of the music.

To make matters worse, the people in the tent joined in on the fun by clapping and cheering frequently. After intubating the patient, I heard cymbals crash and the audience cheer. When we got the IV, the crowd went wild. Drums drummed, cymbals crashed, people cheered—all unaware that just outside the tent, we sat trying to save a man's life.

The moment was surreal, to say the least.

As I knelt there in the field, intubating the patient and trying to get the CPR to go right, hearing people cheer and the percussion ring out, I couldn't help but laugh. Knowing this to be problematic, as I did not wish to offend the family standing nearby, I decided it was time to get the patient onto a backboard and into the ambulance.

On the way to the medical clinic, CPR continued, and weirdly enough, so did the patriotic music because my partner and I found that "The Monkey Wrapped His Tail Around the Flagpole" was the perfect patriotic song for CPR. We continued treatment for the few miles it took to get to Keystone Clinic, singing the whole way.

What do we do to cope?

Everyone has different coping mechanisms that help them get through tough times. Some exercise obsessively, while others may drink excessively. Some want time alone, while others need someone they can talk with about what they are going through. Each one of us has a routine under stress, whether we are aware of it or not. This routine lightens the pressure and allows the body to absorb the stress without it overwhelming the senses.

Humor was always my coping mechanism as an emergency responder. I joke and laugh at the most inappropriate times. I often start laughing when I'm at a funeral. I make bad jokes that cause the normal human to look at me with shock and disgust. They don't know me, so they don't understand that it is a stress response. Many in the field of emergency services react with humor to get through the events of each shift. Without it, each day's events would become unbearable.

After particularly tough calls, it is common for crews to get together for a meal. We talk, we laugh, we process. Years ago, after a call involving a death, a group of paramedics and I got together at a Chinese restaurant for lunch. During the meal, we talked about that call, as well as other recent ones. The lunch devolved into one funny story after another, with everyone at the table laughing loudly.

At one point, I looked around, past our large group, and noticed the shocked faces of the people at nearby tables. The civilians. It is so easy to forget when with fellow emergency responders that our experiences aren't exactly polite lunchroom conversation.

After years in this business, this stress reaction, and my typical response to any emergency or large-scale disaster, has led me to question my capacity for compassion. The Dalai Lama was able to forgive and have compassion for the Chinese, who forcefully took away his country and everything he held dear, causing him to live his life in exile. I really don't think I could do that.

I do believe I *feel* compassion. I feel the weight of sorrow when a loved one dies. I feel empathy for those who struggle. But I continue to struggle with forgiveness, and I continue to struggle with knowing where the lines are drawn between compassion and carrying the burden of another's troubles for them. Isn't strength a form of compassion as well? When working with addicts, it doesn't help them to take on their troubles and continue to give when they take. In many cases, it is best to allow people to stand up on their own. The trouble is knowing when the time is right to do this. When is it best to stay, and when is it best to let go?

The other prevalent coping mechanism is the fight, flight, or freeze response. As mentioned previously, I have lived most of my life with my amygdala calling the shots. When my father would come home drunk, I would often freeze and become as small as possible. While playing pool a few years ago, a fight broke out and before I had time to think about it, I found myself outside, shaking. I had automatically fled the scene even though the fight wasn't anywhere near me, and I wasn't in danger. It was a trauma response developed over time.

The first time I tried therapy, I was wholly unprepared. I knew that something from my past was holding me back, but I also did not wish to relive anything from my past that I had subconsciously hidden as a protective mechanism. I mean, it was protecting me, right? Why would I wish to remember? So, I sought out someone that claimed they could help me release old traumas without having to actually remember what those traumas were—win-win!

What ended up happening, however, was that I burst into tears in every session without knowing why, and I wanted to run out of the room as soon as the therapist asked the first question. I also felt more and more vulnerable with each session, leading to my last session, where I ended up hiding in my house with the doors locked and window shades all drawn, lying in the fetal position on the floor. I left that session feeling as if all my energy had been drained from my body. I was empty. I just wanted to get out of there and get home where I had always felt secure.

On my way home, which was only about five miles from the therapist's office, I noticed that a large truck with a busted front bumper was tailing me. The truck would rev its engine, get within a foot of my bumper, and then back off again. Now, typically when someone does this to me, I slam on my brakes—it works like a charm to get assholes off my bumper.

But on this day, I didn't react with confidence or anger. Instead, my heart started racing, and my palms began to sweat. I felt exposed and defenseless. To make matters worse, the truck mirrored every turn I made. If I turned left, it turned left immediately behind me. I even circled the block a few times. The truck followed. At this point, I couldn't go home—I was terrified. Instead, I picked up my phone and called 911 to report that I was being followed. As soon as the truck noticed me on the phone, the driver veered away and headed in the opposite direction.

I drove around for a bit, still uneasy about going home, but after some time, I finally turned onto my road and drove my car quickly into the garage and shut the door. I was absolutely certain that the man in the truck knew exactly where I lived and was merely waiting for me to let my guard down. I quickly ran room to room, checking all the windows and doors to ensure they were secure. I also had three dogs at the time—a rottweiler, a pit bull mix, and an Australian cattle dog. But even with all of that combined, I was freaked. I closed every blind and hid on the floor along the wall, near the front window, waiting.

I sat there for maybe an hour with my dogs until I felt secure enough to get up, go to my bedroom with my dogs and lock the door. The next morning, I chalked it all up to my energy being so low after therapy. I called and quit therapy then and there.

Sometimes running away is the right thing to do, but sometimes it is best to stay and face the conflict head-on. I am more aware now of each coping mechanism and how they help or harm. I work to increase the helpful coping mechanisms, such as a bit of humor in sad situations, and decrease the activities that do not serve me. This has taken courage over the years and has helped me work through some of the worst traumas of my past.

During my forties, my health problems caused me to evaluate my coping mechanisms once again and to determine a healthy path forward. Within those ten years, I had been admitted twice to the hospital for blood clots in my lungs, a blood clot in my leg, and two hospitalizations for an ulcer. So, when the ER doctor told me in 2018 that I had a kiwi-sized mass in the center of my chest, nestled between both lungs, my heart, and my spine, I was only somewhat surprised.

My forties were kicking my ass!

The pulmonologist came to see me in the emergency room. "I can't believe that no one ever told you about this," he said after introductions. "Something like this needs to be found quickly so that it can be treated." He seemed more upset than I was at learning about the mass in my chest.

"If this was lung cancer," he continued, "you wouldn't be sitting here today. Other symptoms would have developed, or you would be dead by now." He was visibly irritated, especially with the knowledge that I had come into the hospital multiple times and had multiple tests and scans in that period.

He referred me to a cardiothoracic surgeon, who was a bit of an odd duck—but most of the really good surgeons are, so I was comfortable with his style. And the doctor made me laugh, so I knew we'd get along just fine.

The next few months consisted of a series of procedures to find out what the hell the mass was that had been putting pressure on my pulmonary artery, causing chest pain. The physician thought a needle biopsy would give us information about the type of mass and whether it was benign or malignant.

To make matters worse, I had developed a severe allergic reaction to surgical glues and medical adhesives over the years in and out of the hospital, so not only was I nervous about the procedure, but I was also not looking forward to the side effects after the procedure, including welts, redness, hives, and in some cases, burns on my skin from the medical equipment.

Due to the location of the mass on my trachea at the carina (where the trachea divides into two bronchi leading to the lungs), the surgeon performed a transcarinal needle aspiration biopsy typically used to determine lung cancer. The procedure was outpatient, and I was back home in a few hours. Unfortunately, the surgeon told me that I was one of the 5 percent of patients where the needle biopsy was inconclusive. Therefore, another procedure was scheduled, and another month would go by without an answer.

The next procedure was a mediastinoscopy with biopsy. This method calls for a lighted tube to be inserted through the neck to allow for tissue removal. The surgeon made an incision at the base of my throat, where a tube was inserted and moved down to the bifurcation of the trachea. An incision was made through my trachea into the mass to provide the physicians and the lab with a sample to examine.

As soon as I woke from the anesthesia, the surgeon told me that the test was once again inconclusive. He said that the mass had a hard shell around it, making it difficult to get a good-sized sample. He was unable to determine whether it was a tumor or whether it was benign or malignant. I'd have to come back again for the more invasive surgical procedure called a video assisted thoracoscopic surgery. I headed into December without knowing what lay ahead for the new year.

During these months of uncertainty, I examined all the ways I cope with uncertainty and trauma. In and out of the hospital, with every test coming up as inconclusive, was incredibly frustrating. I really just wanted to know what it was so that I could develop a plan, but the universe had other ideas in mind. I believe now that I needed that time to evaluate my life, my fears, my connections to others, and my thoughts about what comes next.

I learned during that time that I am comfortable with my own death. I had allowed myself to be ruled by fear over the years, but when faced with the ultimate end, those fears evaporated like an early morning fog. If the diagnosis came back poor, I would be able to manage it. I would find a positive way to cope.

PHASE 4:
ACCEPTING

Deadheads deal with adversity by remembering that when they've done all there is to do, there's nothing left to do but smile, smile, smile.

—Jerry Garcia

CHAPTER 21

Connection

WE RESPONDED TO a call at Arapahoe Basin Ski Resort to pick up an injured skier who had broken his femur. I worked with an EMT that day, so I knew I would be attending the patient due to the extent of his injuries. As we arrived and stepped out of the ambulance, I noticed how much the weather had changed. In less than an hour, the snow had changed from a light dusting to large, heavy flakes pouring from the sky.

When we arrived at the first-aid station, I found our patient, a young man with dark brown hair, lying on a backboard talking with the ski patrol personnel. At first glance, he didn't look critical. He had been wearing a helmet, there were no visible injuries, and he was alert and answering questions appropriately. But something told me that all was not as it seemed.

I learned that he had been skiing down a slope when he went off a jump and hit a tree in midair. Knowing this, I also knew that any number of injuries might be hidden beneath the skin, and we wouldn't know the full story until we got him to a clinic or hospital for further scans. I tried to get an initial blood pressure but was unable to hear anything. I tried for a distal pulse but could not feel a pulse. The femur fracture was no longer my greatest concern.

We loaded the patient into the ambulance and began to drive to Keystone Ski Resort, where there was a clinic open that could stabilize the patient and determine the next steps for patient care. I noticed that the snow had picked up while we were working inside. I asked my partner to call dispatch and request the Terra 2 Flight for Life ground ambulance, a critical care ambulance that includes a flight nurse and is used when the helicopter cannot fly due to weather. Something told me that every minute was going to count. The snow intensified, slowing our drive down the mountain pass into Keystone.

I tried a few more times to get a set of vitals to no avail. Instead, I switched my efforts to getting two large IV lines in both arms to secure access for fluids and medications. If the patient truly had no discernible distal pulse or blood pressure, then he would need all the fluids he could get. I called ahead to the clinic, informed them that I activated Terra 2, and told them we were coming in emergent. They were confused because we had all been told this was a stable patient with a femur fracture, but everything was screaming at me to make haste and to get him to a higher level of care as soon as possible.

When we arrived at the clinic, I began my report as we wheeled the patient into one of the trauma rooms, and more than one person gave me a hard time about activating the Flight for Life ambulance, thinking that I was just incompetent and unable to get a blood pressure. After their attempts at vitals, however, their attitude changed. And after the first scans were reviewed by the trauma physician on duty, everyone agreed that this patient needed to get to a Denver area hospital as soon as possible. He had broken all his ribs and was bleeding into his chest. They placed two chest tubes, began pushing both saline and blood, and worked hard to get his pressure to a measurable level. The patient was also extremely cold, and without the blood moving through his system, it was almost impossible to get him warm. Through it all, however, our patient remained awake and alert, answering questions and interacting in a way that contradicted his critical state.

The Terra 2 Flight for Life ambulance arrived, received a report, and began to transfer the patient into the ambulance for the long transport to Denver. On a good day, the transport would take an hour, but this was not a good day. It was late afternoon, so skier traffic back to Denver would be heavy. And the snow continued to fall, creating hazardous driving conditions.

Peter, the flight nurse, popped out of the ambulance before they left and asked me to go with him to Denver. He needed assistance with the patient. I quickly contacted my supervisor, who told me that I couldn't go and that he would find someone else to attend the patient with Peter.

Seriously?

I looked at the back of the ambulance as Peter hurried to get everything ready for the long transport. There was no time to wait. My gut told me I had to go with Peter, so I told my supervisor I had no choice, and I jumped in the back of the ambulance to begin our long journey to St. Anthony's Central Hospital.

Throughout the transport, the patient grabbed my hand whenever there was a chance. In total, we gave him eight additional units of blood, along with an additional thirteen bags of fluid. We ran out of oxygen due to the delay caused by the blizzard conditions and had to stop in Clear Creek County to meet up with another ambulance crew who resupplied us for the second half of our trip. We did all we could to warm him, but the patient's lack of blood kept his temperature dangerously low.

Our patient remained awake and alert throughout the entire three-hour transport to St. Anthony's, and as we arrived, we wheeled him directly to T-2, a specialized trauma room that also worked as an operating room. Within minutes, our patient was given anesthesia, and the surgeons opened him up to begin the hard work of fixing what was broken.

The patient ultimately lost a kidney, had a fractured spleen and liver, broke multiple bones throughout his body, and had severe internal bleeding. Everything worked against him on that day. His injuries did not look serious, leading to possible delays in appropriate diagnosis. He was injured in an area that led to a long transport by ski patrol and later by ambulance to a trauma center in Keystone, and his transport had been delayed by both heavy end-of-day skier traffic and a blizzard that moved into the area late that afternoon. But even though all the chips looked to be against him, our patient showed us his strength throughout the process. We each worked in our own way to save his life, from the ski patrollers to the flight nurse to the doctors at both the clinic and hospital. But it was ultimately the patient who held on through it all. He later told Peter, the flight nurse, that as he held my hand, he was literally sucking my life force from me to survive.

This patient had a long recovery, but ultimately, he did recover. And he was later featured in *Life* magazine as an example of someone who defied all the odds to live another day.

MOST OF MY life, I have sought connection.

There is an old Norse belief that everything is connected to everything else. When you affect one area, you impact all other areas, good and bad. All living things are part of this large web of energy that ebbs and flows. If one strand is cut, the rest of the web keeps everything together until new connections can form. An action by one person sends ripples scattering from that person in concentric circles, causing others to also act.

The first time I really felt this was when I was an extra in the 1991 movie *Honeymoon in Vegas* with Nicolas Cage and Sarah Jessica Parker. During the filming, we spent an entire day in the back of a showroom playing cards while cameras rolled in front of us. There was a guy at our table who was a scholar—a professor, I think—who was kind and funny. He was also a bit odd. I felt a connection to him immediately. A strong connection. I met him and spoke with him for one day of my life, but even twenty-five years later, I remember how strong of a connection I felt to that one person.

I recently asked a group of paramedics what they thought of when asked about connection. One talked about the connection he had with his paramedic partner. They had worked together for several years and no longer had to speak to clearly understand what the other needed when treating a patient. He described a rhythm or dance that the two had created after so much time working together. Another paramedic mentioned a call he went on involving the death of an eight-year-old child. Both parents had functioning autism but didn't seem to understand what had occurred. The paramedic crew conducted CPR on the child and talked to the parents throughout, ensuring they were informed of everything the crew was doing to try to revive the child and even transported the parents with the child, allowing them the support of the staff upon arrival at the hospital. The parents would come to appreciate the extra care that the crew had taken.

Yet another story involved a call with a woman having chest pain. She coded while the crew was on scene, they shocked her and brought her back. They transported her and got her to the Cath Lab in time, where the doctors and nurses placed a stent. Since that time, for over nine years, the paramedic's family and her family still get together for holidays and family gatherings.

I could relate to each of these stories—the one patient that stays with you forever, the families that are impacted by tragedy only to unite during the crisis, and the comfort that is found with just the right partner.

While working as a paramedic, I felt deeply connected to a small group of other medics—the nature of the job creates a close connection to those you work with regularly. Twenty-four-hour shifts, stressful calls, and life-and-death situations will do that. The people I worked with became my family—just as dysfunctional as my first family but much more fun.

The strong connections I have had with people in my life can be counted on one hand. After learning to make myself smaller and disappear when uncomfortable, it has been difficult to go back to a place where I can be seen and can connect with others. Instead, when I get too close to people, I tend to panic a bit, and I find a reason to run away. I did this with a few men who seemed to want to get close and start a relationship. I did this with friends who disappointed me or made me feel as if they may not stay. Instead of waiting around, I disconnected completely.

There has been only one time in my life where I have failed at this.

When my mother moved out of state during my last year in high school, I moved into a townhouse with roommates until we graduated. One roommate was a twenty-one-year-old named Rob West, who was a really good friend of my brother's and who became a stabilizing force in the house. The other roommate was Tammie. Her mother had recently decided to move away, and Tammie did not have a place to go, so we became roommates and connected immediately.

In my late twenties, at a time when we were getting on one another's nerves, I thought that maybe she really didn't want to be around anymore. We were arguing a lot. My old habits returned and during one phone call, I said, "Maybe we should just take a break from each other for a while." I felt that pressure building in my chest again, telling me to flee before she decided to end our friendship.

"Friends don't take a break!" she said tersely. "They stay. They work things out! Don't ever say something like that to me again."

She was just so irritated at me. I don't know that I have ever heard her so upset. Even though she may not have known it at the time, that one action made all the difference in my life. Tammie is the one person in my entire life that would not allow me to run. And through the years, she has kept me firmly tethered to this world with her kindness and her ability to make me feel connected to others. She stayed.

She is, and will always be, my person.

I realize that I have always been drawn to others who lack connections. I tend to understand the misfits and outcasts more than the mainstream. I get why people wish to create a new path instead of traveling along the path that everyone else is walking. And if just one action leads to a better connection for those in need, then I am willing to reach out. It only takes one connection to keep people moving forward.

CHAPTER 22

HOPE

"**Can you help** him?" The little boy looked up at my partner and me with such sadness in his eyes.

We had responded to a vehicle rollover accident on Loveland Pass. The vehicle had hit the guardrail, spun around, and slid off the road. Upon arrival, we found a young family with mom, dad, and a five-year-old boy. All were out of the car and walking around—nothing but a few bumps and bruises from the accident.

"You have to help him," the kid said to his dad.

I looked at the father. "Is someone else injured?" I asked. We had already checked out the vehicle, and no one else was inside.

"No," the father said. "Everyone is fine."

The boy pointed to the side of the road. "He is over there. I saw him. He's injured."

He sounded so distraught, so I leaned down, followed his arm with my eyes, and told him I would go check it out. My partner and I walked over to the other side of the road and found an injured dog lying in the snow next to the trees. The boy broke free from his dad and ran toward us. His father followed and grabbed him before he got too close. I had no idea where the dog had come from, but he looked like he had been hit by a car. His fur was bloody next to his right hind leg, and he obviously couldn't walk.

"Please, Dad," the son said again quietly, "we have to help him."

After examining the dog for a few moments, my partner and I looked at the young boy with hope in his eyes and then looked back at one another.

What the hell.

I knelt next to the boy and told him we would do everything possible to help the dog. My partner and I returned with the gurney, carefully loaded the dog up, and wheeled him back to the ambulance. The boy still looked nervous, but he smiled at us both once the dog was safely in the back of the ambulance.

The boy's father mouthed, "Thank you," as we cleared the scene and drove to the veterinary clinic in town. I am happy to say the dog made a full recovery.

―⚞―

WHENEVER I THINK about hope, I cannot help but remember the story of Pandora's Box. For those who don't know the story, Zeus had a daughter named Pandora, and she was sent to Earth as the first woman. After a Titan named Prometheus stole fire from heaven and gave it to humans, Zeus took revenge on humankind by giving Pandora a box with the warning not to open it, knowing full well she would. She was very curious, so one day, she stole the key from her husband and opened the box. Out flew ghostly forms, all the evils known to man, and they spread throughout the earth. As soon as Pandora realized what she had done, she quickly closed the box. The whole contents had escaped, except for one thing. At the very bottom of the box was the spirit of Hope.

The question that has plagued many is why hope was in a box full of evil. Is hope good, or is it bad? Some believe that hope is evil because it leads to disillusionment. Some believe that Zeus put hope into the box to keep humans going so that they would suffer longer and more terribly. With hope, people continue to go on through horrible circumstances. Therefore many believe that hope is the worst of all evils.

Others believe that hope being trapped at the bottom of the box expresses the belief that if you hold onto hope, all will never be lost. People believe that hope is good, and it allows people to overcome evil.

If you look at science, it shows that hope and optimism can mitigate torment. People who are optimistic tend to live happier and healthier lives. On the other hand, the effects of hope and optimism can depend on the specific contents of the hopeful belief. If you hope for things that cannot possibly happen, then you are dooming yourself to unanswered dreams and disillusionment.

When trying to determine my beliefs about whether hope is good or evil, I turn to two books as examples. The first is the book, *Unbroken* by Laura Hillenbrand, which is the true story of Louis Zamperini. The part of the story that hit me the most was when he and ten of his crew crashed their plane into the sea during WWII. Only three survived the crash and had to live on a lifeboat for over forty-seven days. Two of the crew, including Zamperini, continued to believe that they would be rescued and did whatever possible to survive. The third crew member was in despair from the beginning of their ordeal and continually talked about how they would never survive, and all hope was lost. Out of the three crew members, this man was the only one to die. Zamperini and his other crew member that held onto hope survived. This same moral has been seen again and again in true stories of survival and resilience.

The other book is *Gone with the Wind*, written by Margaret Mitchell. My old roommate, Julian, read this book and was just horrified at how awful Scarlett O'Hara was to everyone around her. She was selfish, materialistic, and egotistical. But what he didn't see was that it was Scarlett who got everyone through the war and into recovery. If it weren't for her strength, determination, and, yes, hope, the entire family would have perished.

Margaret Mitchell was interviewed once and asked what made her write this novel. She said she wanted to tell the story of the differences between those who are survivors and those who are victims. Some just lie down and give up when faced with terrible events. But others, like Scarlett, continue to pick themselves up, brush themselves off, and move forward. Scarlett was a survivor, just like Louis Zamperini, and both had the one thing considered by some to be an evil in the world—they had hope.

Are you one of those who believes hope is among the world's worst evils, or do you remain optimistic about the future and believe hope will get you through? For me, I tend to be a glass is half full kind of girl, so I must believe that when Pandora opened the box and only hope was left behind, it signaled that if we hold onto hope, we will make it through whatever may come our way.

CHAPTER 23

Chaos

"**Man, it's been** a hell of a shift."

My partner looked worn out. We'd been running since the shift began at 7 a.m., and we had just gotten back to our quarters for the first time in fourteen hours.

"Well, the good news is that skier traffic has slowed," I said, trying to be positive. "I'm going to fix some dinner real quick before our next call."

I walked into the kitchen and pulled a few things out of the refrigerator, thinking about the day and hoping we had seen the worst. A minute later, my partner entered the living area, sat down on the couch, and turned on the television.

BEEP BEEP BEEP BEEP BEEP

"Ambulance Three, Dispatch."

I picked up the radio while simultaneously grabbing my food and putting it back in the fridge. "Go ahead for Ambulance Three."

"Ambulance Three respond to Eastbound I-70 Mile Marker 210 for the report of a man running down the freeway. Reports are that the man is on fire."

"Well, shit," I said calmly before getting back on the radio. "Ambulance Three enroute."

We both moved quickly back downstairs to the ambulance, my partner getting into the driver's side and me getting into the back to get some equipment prepared.

As he pulled out of the bay, I leaned into the driver's compartment. "Think of it this way," I said to my partner. "There is at least one person that is definitely having a worse day than we are."

―⚔︎―

I HAVE A systems brain. I am also an empath and intuitive. These traits have allowed me to feel connection on an individual and a universal scale. I see the strings connecting individuals and see the bands that tie them together.

Darkness and Light.

Yin and Yang

The Force and the Dark Side.

It is the network of energy that binds us all—the connection to something larger and more powerful. It is quantum physics, baby!

I believe in science, but I also believe in magic. I believe in medicine, but I also believe in the power of the mind to heal. I believe in that which I can see and understand, but also in the unknown. It is all around us—this energy that connects us all together.

My interest in this large web of life, and possibly my search for connectedness, led me into the field of complexity theory and chaos theory several years back. I once read about a study on connectedness and disasters. Researchers at Princeton University believe that so many people were impacted around the world by the events of 9/11 that their collective energy altered the operation of computers. Think about that. Carl Yung taught us about the collective unconscious, but this research illustrates a collective consciousness where the energy shifted to such an extent that computers stopped functioning as predicted. This was called the Global Consciousness Project, and since 9/11, these results have been replicated during other large-scale disasters, illustrating the power of collective energy.

I first heard of complexity theory at the Naval Postgraduate School in Monterey, California, while attending the Center for Homeland Defense and Security as part of the Executive Leaders Program. I was instantly intrigued. Once I returned home, I read as much as I could about it and subsequently became a student of chaos theory. It is now deeply ingrained in all that I do in my work. More importantly, it ultimately freed me from my fears and anxieties related to my work as an emergency manager.

In popular culture, most know chaos theory as the "butterfly effect"—you know, the one where a butterfly flaps its wings in Australia and it causes a typhoon in another part of the world. But what I learned in my reading is that it is just a bit more complicated than that.

When I first entered the emergency management field, there weren't a lot of plans or examples to build from. Emergency management was in its infancy. I learned as I went and created a program based on what I believed was most needed. But I also worried all the time about the unknowns. There was so much that could go wrong, so many scenarios that could happen, how could I possibly be ready for them all? For years, I worked to learn all I could about the field, and I pushed myself to try to understand everything that would be needed to best respond to a large-scale disaster, but in the back of my head, the worry remained.

The study of chaos theory finally freed me. From that point forward, I was able to settle into the field, and I found a new way of thinking about disasters. The first thing I learned is that no one, and I mean no one, can plan for every eventuality. It is impossible. Multiple military leaders going all the way back to Sun Tzu, Clausewitz, and Moltke have been attributed to some variation of the quote, "No plan survives first contact with the enemy." This is because the minute you execute your plan, its success is dependent upon outside factors—connected technology, weather, the environment, terrain, and even the reactions of the people involved. So how can anyone expect to have all the answers to every question?

Learning this one thing allowed me to let go of the idea that I could control anything. Instead, I learned how to move with the changes. I learned how to adapt in real time to what is going on and to see the interconnections between all things. This helped me both in my work and in my personal life. Chaos theory brought together all the seemingly disparate ideas and theories I had knocking around in my head. I am an empath who picks up on the energy around me. I am intuitive, sensing things before they happen. I am a systems thinker who sees interconnections among systems, networks, people, and communities. And my Viking blood tells me that all living things are interconnected.

Knowing how and why people react as they do is related to their interconnections with others. When people are in crisis, everything is chaos—they cannot see answers and cannot move forward. Instead, they react. In that reaction, they can make things much worse, or they can get to a point where a specific reaction leads them to something more manageable—maybe they are able to recognize their situation from other known situations they have faced before. If this happens, they can begin to slowly move out of chaos to a sense of order.

When I am in crisis, I know that I just need to give it a bit more time. I don't always need to react. Sometimes, I need to slow things down and watch. Thoughts slow, patterns emerge, and eventually, I see the path forward—I move out of the dark into the light. It allows me to avoid slipping off the cliff into chaos.

I learned to stop trying to predict what might happen because prediction is impossible. I learned that although prediction is not possible, there are patterns that we can work from. The complex systems we work in every day in the field of emergency management are also systems that self-organize, adapt, and change as we respond to them, so our plans and processes must adapt as well. Nothing is static. It is all interconnected.

Connection goes beyond one individual connected to another. Connection is broader and so much more important in the grand scheme. Every action I take will have an impact on others, and therefore, I must live a life of honor, character, and generosity.

I must live a life that is worthy.

CHAPTER 24

Eyes Wide Open

It was another cold, snowy night on Loveland Pass in the mountains of Colorado. The roads were icy, and another unsuspecting driver slid first one way and then the other, finally colliding with an oncoming traveler. When I arrived with the fire engine and my crew, we got to work. There were two people in one vehicle, and both needed to be extricated from the vehicle since it was munched up around them. To make matters worse, the driver of the vehicle had a major head injury—causing him to be combative. So, after removing the passenger from the vehicle, it was determined that the only way to get the driver out was to peel back the roof of the vehicle. Therefore, my roommate and member of my fire crew, Julian, entered the passenger side to hold the patient steady to protect his neck. But since the patient was combative, the patient continually struck Julian in the head while he tried to save the patient's life.

Yes, the glamorous world of firefighting.

Meanwhile, I worked to get medicine out of the ambulance that had just arrived so that we could calm the patient enough to remove him from the vehicle. As I grabbed the syringe and turned back to the car, I saw that the firefighters were swinging an ax down onto the roof of the vehicle to create the crease that was needed to peel back the roof and extricate the patient. I also noticed Julian's head just below the ax inside the car.

"Everybody stop!" I yelled, waving my arms at the firefighter with the ax. This was one of many times when I saw the true harm of tunnel vision. Everyone was doing their individual job, but no one was looking at the scene as a whole.

"You are about to give Julian a killer headache," I said, gesturing into the car. He and his patient were at risk of getting their heads bashed in with an ax with the current plan.

The firefighter with the ax bent down and looked inside the vehicle at Julian. "Sorry, dude," he said with a shrug.

A quick change of plan and a bit of medication to calm the combative patient allowed us to safely remove him and load him into the ambulance. We loaded our equipment back up into the engine and headed back to the station to our now very cold and not-too-tasty dinner.

I WOKE UP today thinking of Jerry Garcia and my years in Las Vegas after high school, where I spent a great deal of time at Grateful Dead shows, living like a hippie. I cannot help but feel deep peace and smile a big ole smile when I think of my time listening to the Dead. And whenever I think about the Grateful Dead, I think about all the wonders of the universe and all that my eyes have seen.

Once your eyes have been opened, it is impossible to erase what they have seen. You can close your eyes again, but the images become a part of your dreams or thoughts. This is good, and it is bad. The bad is obvious—when you see traumatic events or read about something horrific, such as trying to save a life, it will stay with you. It may haunt you or disrupt your sleep. When I read the book *Roots* by Alex Haley, I had nightmares for weeks, and I still can visualize the slave ships—and this was just from reading a book. Imagine the difference when you actually live it.

This is why many live their lives with their heads in the sand. They would much rather not see or hear or touch the bad. If they don't know about it, then it cannot harm them. My mom once told me that her generation would much rather not talk about the bad times and forget they happened, whereas my generation tends to swim around in the bad times to examine them fully.

My first brush with therapy was an absolute trainwreck. I tried to power through my trauma without trying to understand it. I tried to let go of fear without knowing what caused the fear. I was trying to take the easy way out. All the benefits and none of the consequences. Of course, it was a total disaster.

The second time I tried therapy, I went into it more secure and with my eyes wide open. I no longer wanted to hide from my past. I wanted to know—everything. If something terrible had happened, I wanted to know about it and work through it. I found out quickly that I couldn't just force myself to plow through the trauma, dust off my hands, and move on to a happy, carefree life. I learned that it is a process and that I have to be willing to take the time, swim around in the trauma a bit, and maybe even learn to live with it and accept it as part of who I am.

Sometimes I feel that therapy is nothing more than me paying someone a lot of money to sit and talk. Maybe I can just pay a stranger to have a cup of coffee with me and talk to them instead? It would be a lot less costly, that's for sure. But other times, I come away with one thought or idea that seems to be profound—possibly a breakthrough. Of course, I am still at the beginning of this journey, but I now understand that it is a process, not an end state.

In one session, I started by discussing the sexual assault in my twenties, not going into any details but using it as an example of a time in my life when I did not stand up for myself. Time and again, I let people walk on me, abuse me, treat me like trash. I just let them. I told my therapist that it is this that bothers me most about my past—not necessarily the actions of others, but the fact that I didn't defend myself in any way. In most cases, I walked away without saying a word.

This led to a conversation about how we are born with our whole selves—who we fundamentally are as human beings. Over time, pieces of that self, called exiles, break away, floating alone without the ability to reconnect. These are burdens or pains and traumas. In response to this, we establish protectors, which attach to the exiles. These are the coping mechanisms we create to deal with trauma. For example, I work in a field that is all about preparing for the bottom to drop out. This could very well be a protective mechanism that was created from a childhood where the bottom constantly fell out. I learned how to protect myself by building up tools to prepare for whatever may come my way. I built up protectors to manage my fears.

The most interesting part of all this was when we started to talk about the protectors. I mentioned that I always picture Donnelly, one of my spirit guides, standing near me, protecting me from harm. I visualize a large Scottish Highlander with a long sword always standing by my side, willing to take out anyone who comes to harm me. I also often call on the Archangel Michael when I feel vulnerable or when I feel I need protection. He, too, holds a long sword and wears armor as the ultimate protector.

During this specific session, my therapist mentioned that over time, the goal is to decrease the need for the protectors in their attachment to the exile traumas. She asked me about telling Donnelly maybe to stop protecting me for a while. Without delay, I began shaking my head back and forth, and I burst into tears. The thought of not having Donnelly or Michael there to protect me made me instantly fearful and extremely vulnerable. I had never thought about how much I depended upon that vision of protection, but I won't forget how I felt when she suggested I let go of some of that protection. I was terrified, with no real idea as to why.

But here's the thing. Although I didn't quite understand the reaction, it was a key to unlocking the past. I feel an overwhelming need for protection from harm. From something. Knowing this allows me to think more about what it is that causes me such fear, which may help me let that fear go.

I believe in keeping my eyes wide open to capture the good with the bad. There are those who want us to forget the Holocaust ever happened, but imagine the lessons that would be lost if we closed our eyes to those who died in concentration camps during WWII or the internment camps for Japanese Americans. When we bury our heads in the sand, we repeat our mistakes over and over again. And while life would often be much easier or more enjoyable if I were able to keep my eyes closed to all that is going on around me, I wouldn't be part of the solution because I would never fully recognize the problem.

This brings me to the true gift of keeping your eyes open to the world around you. It brings wonder into your existence. I will look at something such as a carpet in a bedroom. Who would have thought of something like that? Maybe after too many nights with freezing feet and no way to warm them they invented a rug and then thought, "Well, I might as well just cover the whole floor instead of just this small space, then my feet will never get cold." These are the things that keep me up at night—the wonder of the universe and the amazing brilliance of every invention. And it just intensifies further when I read about the universe from someone like Stephen Hawking or when I stand in Italy looking up at the Sistine Chapel and think about Michelangelo's vision and drive. Too many people are too busy to take the time to pay attention to the wonder of a sunrise or the joy of a dog with a newfound bone. I have those moments like others where life is so busy I let the wonder pass me by. And then I have a day like today where I woke up and read a magazine article about the Grateful Dead, and it took me back to summer days in a lawn chair with a beer in my hand and music in my ears, where absolutely everything was perfect, and the wonder of the universe was all around me.

This lesson of awareness has helped me in all areas of my life and continues to help me cope with whatever challenges come my way. It is also something I wish to enhance and study and learn more about so that I can truly be aware of everything and everyone in my life. It will help to teach me what really matters and teach me how to best expend my energy to leave a positive mark on this world. That awareness also keeps my perspective clear. Do I really need to worry about that coworker who gets mad over the tone of an email? Do I need to let it ruin my day when my dog destroys my journal for the *second* time in a week like she did today? No! Instead, I can have a yelling party in my bedroom closet all alone and come out to hug my dog and tell her how much I love her because that is what truly matters. It is all about perspective.

Those who choose to live life with their heads in the sand or with their eyes closed to the tragedies of the world may believe they are protected and safe. They may believe their life is complete. But it is just an illusion. They are unable to truly see the wonders of the world. Without the bad, they cannot experience the truly grand. I feel great joy because I have experienced utter sadness. And I wouldn't give up those moments of joy or sadness for anything in the world.

Thank you, Jerry, for the reminder today.

CHAPTER 25

TIME

"Ambulance Three, respond to mile marker 204 for the report of a two-vehicle collision with injuries."

"Ambulance Three enroute."

Upon arrival, we parked the ambulance in a safe location near the engine and got out to assess the scene. A firefighter walked up to us as we got closer.

"There are no injuries," he said, "but there is a body in that car over there." He pointed to the Suburban nearby.

"What do you mean there is a body in the car? You just said there are no injuries."

"The coroner's body is in the car."

"The coroner's body?"

"Yes, his body is in that car."

"Are you telling me that Dave's body is in that car?" Dave was the county coroner, and he also happened to be an EMT on the ambulance service in Summit County.

"Yes."

"But I just saw Dave this morning," I said, confused, as I started toward the Suburban. "Are you sure it is Dave?"

"No, no, no," the firefighter said, running to catch up, waving his arms. "Not Dave himself. The body in the back of the Suburban belongs to the coroner," he explained. "The woman died earlier today, and one of the deputy coroners was taking her to the funeral home when the Suburban was struck by that truck over there." He pointed over his shoulder at the other vehicle.

"So there really is a body in the back of that Suburban, and it really is the coroner's body?"

The firefighter laughed. "Yes."

The next day, an editorial appeared in the newspaper from Dave, the county coroner, titled, "News of my death has been greatly exaggerated."

Time.

We know from the day that we are born that we are on limited time. We just don't know if it will be days, weeks, or years. As an emergency responder, I was reminded of that ticking clock on every call.

One common thread for anyone in emergency services is the number of near misses we all face. Most calls are benign, maybe a transport from one facility to another, or a thousand different car accidents in bad weather with no injuries. But sometimes, there would be that call that would remind you of the dangers of the job—the near misses where if the circumstances had changed just a little bit, you would become the next casualty.

When traveling up from Denver on I-70 headed back to Summit County, our ambulance traveled west and headed down Floyd Hill to the big curve at the bottom. At the same time, heading east, was a semitruck traveling downhill out of control. When the semi reached the curve, it tipped its entire load over the median into the oncoming westbound traffic lane, spilling frozen dinners all over the freeway. Our ambulance had missed the accident by a mere quarter mile, turning the corner and heading uphill just as the semi traveled down the hill and rolled.

On another occasion, traveling along I-70 westbound at 1 a.m., transferring a patient from Summit Medical Center to Vail Valley Hospital, I drove as my partner attended the patient in the back of the ambulance. As I drove, I saw headlights that looked to be coming our way, but on the freeway, headlights should not have been seen on that stretch of highway. The eastbound lanes were far from us and lower in the canyon. But I distinctly saw headlights that seemed to be moving closer as I watched the road. Suddenly, faster than I would have imagined, the car was right in front of the ambulance, heading the wrong way down I-70, in my lane. I swerved at the last moment and just avoided a head-on collision at high speed.

My partner could be heard cussing me out in the back as he ping-ponged around the compartment. "Goddamn it," he yelled, trying to hang on to the railing on the ceiling. "What the hell are you doing?"

"Look out the back window," I yelled back, irritated.

As soon as he saw the taillights of the quickly retreating vehicle fading from view, he calmed and sat back down on the bench seat. "Never mind."

On another occasion, an ambulance was struck along the freeway by another vehicle that saw the pretty flashing lights and decided to drive straight toward them. And again, on I-70, a box-spring mattress flew off a vehicle in front of us, hitting our ambulance grill and ultimately going under the engine compartment, causing us to run over it at high speed. The mattress skidded under the ambulance for several hundred feet before finally dislodging and flinging into another lane.

Those are just the near misses I experienced on the freeway.

They don't include the calls where the patient was under the influence or combative where, if I was not careful, they would kick the shit out of me. It doesn't include the normal dangers of working in a burning building or going into a house containing a meth lab or treating the highly contagious. It doesn't include the domestic violence calls, the active shooter incidents, or those who intentionally wished to harm emergency services personnel. Each day was—and still is—a reminder that time is fleeting, and life is precious. We have a short amount of time to do the things we feel are most important, to possibly do some good in the world, to make a difference.

I often hear that you should live each day as if it were your last. I have to say, I have always hated that. For one, it is impossible to live each day as if it were your last because it might not be, and you still have bills to pay and food to put on the table. If it were my last day, I wouldn't worry about any of that, but if I lived each day like that, I wouldn't have a home or money to do all the other things I would like to do before I die.

Instead, my philosophy is not to wait to do the things you most want or need to do. Make plans now. Go on that trip, see the family members you wish to see, paint that picture, take that walk. Don't wait until retirement to make all your dreams come true—you may not ever get there. Instead of living each day as if it were your last, use each day wisely in the pursuit of your dreams.

When I started having health problems in my forties, people told me I should slow down. I had lived almost fifty years moving fast and thinking fast. I lived as if I might die at any time and knew time was ticking by quickly. Every time someone told me to slow down, I became irrationally angry. Why should I slow down? I like my life, I like my work, and I am just going to keep on going until my end comes and I am going to love every minute of it.

When I returned to therapy, years after my first attempt went horribly awry, I learned more about how the brain works and how trauma wires the brain to react in certain ways. I learned that it was, in large part, my amygdala that kept me moving fast and always on the go.

Just recently, as I have continued to work through my learned behaviors, I realized the beauty in slowing down. I still work fast and think fast, but I also take the time now to purposefully slow things down, look around and see every detail. I send my amygdala on an extended vacation and let the rest of my brain take the lead now and again. We have a short amount of time in this world, so I will continue to explore life while also taking the time to just be here in the present and feel the beauty of each moment. I am pleased to say that when I look back, I see a life well lived. And when I look forward, I see an entire world of opportunity ahead of me. I hope I have the time.

CHAPTER 26

BORN FOR THIS

O N A SUNNY day in July 2011, I drove up the long driveway and parked around the back of the house with the other vehicles. A few tents lined up in a row on the property out in the country in Elbert County. Cory, a local emergency manager, had invited me to attend a summer hog roast at his house, and since I lived at a farmhouse in the same county, it was just a short drive to the party. The sun was high in the sky with nothing but a slight breeze—a perfect summer day.

I found Cory in the crowd and went up to greet him. Cory was tall and built like a football player, a towering presence in any room. He also always had a big smile on his face and a willingness to help those in need. His smile widened when he saw me, and he reached out to shake my hand and greet me. Cory showed me around the house and the property before going back to the rest of his guests.

A short while later, while the guests had just begun getting their food and sitting at picnic tables, clouds moved in quickly, and the slight breeze became a strong wind. Within about ten minutes, the dark, angry clouds had filled the sky, and the winds became so fierce that everyone had to grab what they could from the tables and shelter inside. The rain came quickly, and the wind caused the frame of one of the tents to bend and break the window of a nearby pickup truck. Soon after, the rain turned into hail, pelting the water-soaked earth, bouncing off vehicle roofs and hoods, and causing a cacophony of sound.

I sought shelter in the nearby barn with a bunch of other guests. Water flowed in rivulets across the dirt driveway and around the barn, causing the recently dry dirt roads to become mud bogs.

Cory stood next to me as we watched the freak storm destroy the picnic outside. After a time, he looked around, saw me standing there, and pointed at me. "You, you did this!"

Laughing, I said, "I absolutely did not cause this storm to happen."

"Yes, you did. Everywhere you go, there is chaos." He said, also laughing. "I swear, you are worse than a Stephen King novel."

It is true I have been known as a "black cloud." I have had a long history of having bad events occur in the places I worked.

The year 2012 was billed as the apocalyptic one that would end it all. The Mayan calendar ended in 2012, so many believed that meant the world would end as well (perhaps the Mayans just ran out of energy and figured the calendar had gone far enough—I mean, it had to end at some point). The year started with everyone speculating about when the end would come; we all joked around about the number of conspiracy theories swirling throughout the world, and even Hollywood got on board with a disaster movie only they could imagine.

I thought the year would be bad for an entirely different reason: 2012 was an even year. In Colorado, most of our large wildfire events have occurred in even years. I am a superstitious person, so while I did not believe the world would end, I did believe we were in for a hell of a rough year.

In a severe drought, we all knew that the year would be problematic in terms of wildfires. It hadn't been that dry since 2002 (also an even year), when we had the largest wildfire in Colorado's history. Our office was also going through a massive transition at the state level, so of course we thought that is when we would have the big one.

In the span of forty-five days, I moved from a tornado in Elbert County to the two most destructive fires in Colorado's history to the Aurora theater shooting. In between were several arson fires throughout the Front Range and Western Slope. Oh, and I almost forgot about the meteor shower that sent balls of fire from the sky while working one of those wildfires, grounding all aircraft.

It was a weird year. I had started to believe that maybe the Mayans were right—2012 had lived up to its reputation.

I, too, lived up to my reputation as a "black cloud," causing other emergency managers to urge me to go on vacation or, at the very least, to stay home and out of their county.

And they call themselves emergency managers. Sad!

As for me, I love this work. I get excited at the thought of being able to work in an emergency operations center and getting to manage a disaster. It isn't that I hope for catastrophe. As I said at the beginning of this journey, bad things will happen, and when they do, I would just like to be there to help pick up the pieces.

When I had the sudden realization that I should become a paramedic while stopped at that light in Las Vegas, it had felt so right that I uprooted my whole life to move back to Colorado and begin EMT school. I never thought I would become a firefighter, but once I did, I loved every minute of it. Paramedic school soon followed—each piece felt like a part of the plan. It all felt right. But I wasn't called to do any of those things. Instead, each one of those steps gave me the lessons and knowledge I needed to become an emergency manager and to devote my life to my work in coordinating the response to and recovery from disasters.

This, I was called to do.

How do I know this? I know that I was called to the emergency management field because it felt natural from the very beginning. As a firefighter and as a paramedic, I enjoyed the work, loved the people, and felt I could make a difference, but it all was a bit more of a struggle. I think I was good at what I did, but not great. I had a great deal of anxiety that I would fail. Once I became an emergency manager, I felt free. The field made sense to me when it didn't to others, and I could see a clear path of learning and understanding what was most needed to be exceptional in my craft.

And it is a craft.

Second, my brain operates in a way that is uniquely suited for emergency and disaster work. I see multiple connections and paths simultaneously, which helps when trying to solve complex problems. My brain has also developed all of those coping mechanisms to get through trauma and I am able to use all of that to create a successful career. My therapist once told me that I am great at trauma. She meant that my brain had built up protectors and hypervigilance that were used to create a successful career. Now it was literally my job to look for the pitfalls and points of failure. Finally, I know that I was called to this field because I feel it in every cell of my body.

Some call me driven. I feel like I am *being* driven. Since I can remember, I have felt a push to do more with my talents and my life. It physically feels as if there is someone standing behind me, pushing me forward. Sometimes I hear a loud clapping in my ears that instantly gets me to pay attention and focus on that which is around me. Other times I have heard a voice clearly providing guidance. Most of the time, though, I know I need to do something but don't know a clear path. This is what life is about—getting guidance but finding our own way.

I loved being a firefighter, and I loved being a paramedic. They were both good fields for someone like me who cannot work in a job where each day is the same. I always knew, however, that it wouldn't be my full story. The place I finally found home was in the field of emergency management. I like a fair bit of stress, and I love the chaos that exists during and after a disaster. What I love most is turning that chaos into order; it is a feeling I cannot completely describe, but it is where I find the most joy and feel the most belonging.

I now believe that all my life has been preparing me for the events I have managed and for my work in this incredible field. The push I received from my guides year after year led me to seek excellence and caused me to be uniquely driven in my pursuit to learn and act. The unpredictability of my father in my youth and as a young adult, and my unconventional childhood, led me to plan for any number of eventualities, including the bottom dropping out. I absolutely know bad things will happen to me and those around me. The years in Civil Air Patrol, firefighting, and paramedicine—and my time around death—have allowed me to build up my defenses against the horrors in our world.

I fully understand that waiting for the bottom to fall out—always looking for the shadow around the corner—is not the best way to live. It is a learned behavior that never really leaves you. And in some ways, it has prepared me for my chosen career. But I also now know that it is a trauma response, and it causes internal stress that isn't necessary. A threat doesn't exist around every corner. Living that way is not sustainable.

I wonder if it would be the same if my childhood had been different. I am no longer cowering in the basement, wondering what the night will bring. Instead, I face it head-on with a plan. I learned fear in childhood, but in adulthood, I have learned how to use that to be better prepared for whatever may come my way.

As I look back, the foundational lessons of my life occurred while I worked as a paramedic. This time as a paramedic taught me how to move through chaos and disorder like a river flows over rocks, negotiating the smoothest path possible while encountering the turbulence around me. Although I never felt that it would be my life's path, those years were my learning ground. I became a watcher, I studied human behavior, I learned about deceit as well as kindness, I learned about timing and the energy of a room, and I learned about connection and family. Without those years, I cannot imagine that I would have been ready and able to do what I do today.

I was once told that I have the power within me to walk into a crowd and calm the crowd merely with my presence. I was also told I was only using about 10 percent of my potential. Now, I do not know if any of that is true. I can believe that I still need to work to reach my full potential, but the thought that I should be able to calm others with my presence is awe-inspiring. What I do know, however, is that I would like it to be true. I would like to think that my value to the field of emergency management isn't just knowledge about the field but in my presence and my energy.

Now, when I work in an emergency operations center, I try to start each day with something good—a good story, good news, or just an inspirational quote. We see a lot of the ugly, so it is important to even that out with the beautiful. I would like to think that my presence has the ability to lower the stress level during an incident and that people can count on me to be that orchestra leader, helping to connect all the people and agencies to bring order to the chaos and to bring a bit of light in the dark. This thought brings me great joy. It is what keeps me moving forward.

After the catastrophic year 2020, I no longer feel my guides pushing from behind me. Instead, I feel them standing by my side as I continue to learn and grow. Who knows what lies ahead, but whatever it is, my eyes are wide open, and I am ready.

This is the End

THERE IS NOTHING more heartbreaking than the funeral of a firefighter. It starts with a long procession through town with emergency services vehicles from all neighboring agencies. The firefighter's casket or urn is placed in the back of a fire truck from their home unit and driven through town with people lining the roads to pay their respects. American flags are flown from overpasses, and other emergency services personnel stand in their dress uniforms and salute as the engine goes by. Upon arrival, the pallbearers carry the flag-draped casket into the auditorium lined on both sides by fellow emergency responders.

Many can manage to get through this first part of the service dry-eyed and with a great deal of composure. But then come the bagpipes, which rarely leave anyone without emotion. There is something about the sound that calls people back to mournful times.

Later in the service is the ringing of the bell three times, symbolizing a time when the fire bell rang to call firefighters to an alarm and then, again, to signal that the alarm had ended. This is all hard to get through, along with the eulogy and the stories. But the part of a firefighter funeral that will break the heart of every person in the room is the last radio call.

"Summit Dispatch to Officer Four."

Silence.

"Summit Dispatch to Officer Four."

Again, the most deafening silence you will ever hear.

"Summit Dispatch to Officer Four."

"No response from Officer Four. Officer John Smith answered his last call on Friday, March 5, 2021, at 0900 hours in the line of duty. We thank you for your dedicated service, leadership, and friendship. Rest easy, we have it from here. Dispatch clear."

ON MY LAST full shift as a paramedic for Summit County Ambulance Service, I brought in a forty-nine-year-old male to the Keystone Clinic complaining of chest pain. A few minutes later, ski patrol brought in another forty-nine-year-old male, also complaining of chest pain. He was wheeled in next to my patient. Lying side-by-side, same symptoms, same look, same age.

While writing my report at the nurse's station next to the two gentlemen, the man brought in by ski patrol suddenly coded. He gasped for air, clutched his chest, and lost consciousness—no pulse, no longer breathing. We all ran into the room to help resuscitate the patient. One shock was all it took, and he was back, conscious again and looking frightened.

After all the excitement, I stepped away, and as I moved out of the patient area, I glanced at my patient, who was just a few feet away from the man who had just coded. He didn't just look frightened—he looked terrified. And within just a few moments, his eyes widened, he looked into my eyes, and then he collapsed on the cot, no longer breathing and with no pulse.

Everyone swooped in again and began resuscitation. One shock and, just like his twin next door, his pulse was restored, and he regained consciousness.

Most of my calls with a patient who died ended with the patient still dead. But on my last day as a paramedic, I witnessed not one, but two patients go from dead to alive due to the actions of emergency workers. I considered it a gift as part of a final goodbye to the EMS field.

IN LATE 2018, I went into the emergency room with chest pain and left with the knowledge that I had a kiwi-sized mass growing in my chest. It was situated between both my lungs, wrapped around my trachea, possibly attached to my spine, putting pressure on my pulmonary artery. It had been there for over four years, hiding in plain sight, undetected, and allowed to grow.

From October through December 2018, I had multiple surgical procedures to identify the mass so that the doctors would have a treatment plan. I was referred to a cardiothoracic surgeon who, after multiple additional tests, told me that the mass was "as complicated as it gets."

I had started the decade out vowing it would be my fearless forties, and, in a way, that is exactly what had happened. I had faced multiple life-threatening conditions, time in and out of the hospital, and several unknowns. Through it all, I became more comfortable with myself, my life, and my insecurities. I had faced my ultimate fears. I had taken the challenge and learned something valuable along the way.

I went in for my fourth surgery just before Christmas 2018 thinking it was just the beginning of a long haul and the possibility of multiple surgeries to follow. Prior to the surgery, I visualized two warriors standing at the foot of my bed—Donnelly the Highland warrior and the Archangel Michael, both resting their hands on their swords, which were pointed toward the ground. I felt the need for protection.

When I woke from the surgery, I was in my hospital room, where I would stay for a few more days. When my surgeon came into my room, he had a big smile on his face.

"Did you hear?" he said excitedly.

"No, I have been waiting to hear," I said. "It's good news, though, isn't it?"

"I annihilated that sucker!" he said excitedly. In telling me, he made a sweeping motion with his hands when he talked about excising the mass, a sweeping motion like one used when wielding a sword and swinging it through the air. I thought of the two guardians I had visualized at the end of my bed and sent them my gratitude.

I lifted my arm with my palm facing his direction. "Well done," I said as I high-fived my surgeon, both of us laughing.

Collateral beauty is that beauty that is found rising out of the ashes of catastrophe. It is the magnificent sunrise that only exists because of the smoke from a large wildfire. It is the feeling of belonging to a giving community after surviving a tornado that ravaged your town. It is the memory of a parent staying alive and smiling as she spoke of her life and her children as she worked through her last day battling cancer.

When we consider that bad things will always happen, it is crucially important to keep a lookout for the good in the bad—the collateral beauty that is destined to follow.

This book started out as a series of stories I wanted to capture from my time as a paramedic, but as I wrote, it turned into a reminder about all the lessons I learned from the bad things that happen each day and the things we do to cope. This book is about the moments that truly matter—those that make everything else worthwhile. This is the collateral beauty of catastrophe.

The trauma responses I developed through my childhood and as an early adult helped me to get through the toughest of times. My health troubles in my forties made me examine my life, try to make sense of my fears, and remember that I have a set time on this earth. At the time of that surgery, I felt comfortable with what I had accomplished, and I had time to make arrangements in the event I did not make it through. This was a freeing feeling—knowing all was in order and that I did not fear what was to come.

I have now entered my fifties. I am in a time in my life when I attend more funerals than weddings. But here's the thing—I love this time in my life. My twenties were filled with stupid decisions that really should have killed me along the way. My thirties were spent trying to catch up from the time I thought I had wasted in my twenties. And my forties were about building my career and settling in to being an adult. Now, I can look back at all those years and see them as the learning steps along the way to who I am today. And I like me. I like that I made all those mistakes in my twenties. I like that I built a life I enjoy and a career I love. I like that I have spent time alone and feel comfortable in my own skin. I even like the coping mechanisms I created to deal with trauma. I love that everything bad that has happened in my life has added to who I am as a whole.

As I end this book, I do so with the knowledge that the mass that was removed from my chest has come back and is larger than it was before. The mass is now attached to the back of my heart and possibly my spine. It is difficult to remove. It is complicated. I face mortality once again.

There are many who do not have the privilege of making it to middle age. Their lives are cut short for any number of reasons. All my life, I have thought I would die young, but I have made it to my fifties, and I am going to enjoy the hell out of this time in my life. I am going to find the good in every day. I am going to make some new mistakes. And I am going to continue learning about how chaos can make my life beautiful.

I hope you do the same.

> Stuff your eyes with wonder, he said, live as if you'd drop dead in ten seconds. See the world. It's more fantastic than any dream made or paid for in factories.
>
> —Ray Bradbury, *Fahrenheit 451*

Acknowledgments

I cannot possibly name everyone that has helped me along the way, and who contributed to the calls and lessons I learned that are outlined in this book. I thank all the people who dedicate their careers, and often their lives, to serving others, whether through emergency services and emergency management, through the military or otherwise. Public servants are the ones who have shaped me over the years and who have taught me compassion, empathy, and kindness. I cannot imagine where my life would have led without this wonderful field and all its wonderful people. Thank you for a real good time.

www.ingramcontent.com/pod-product-compliance
Lightning Source LLC
LaVergne TN
LVHW041941070526
838199LV00051BA/2860